ECONOMICS OF ISLAM

[A Comparative Study]

By

Shaikh Mahmud Ahmad

M.A., LL.B

Principal, Government College

Rawlakot (Azad Kashmir)

Peace Publications

42-Manzoor Manzal Urdu-Bazar Lahore

2021
Publish by:
Sayed Zulfiqar Hussan Shah
Peace Publications Lahore

Printed by:
Haji Hanif Printer Lahore, Pakistan

Binder: Qayyum Ahmad

ISBN:969-9988-34-9
ISBN:978-969-9988-34-9

Peace Publications
42.Manzoor Manzal Opp Govt Muslim
Model High School Urdu Bazar Lahore
E-mail:peace_publications@yahoo.com
Cell:0322-4298311-0307-4505020

TO

THE MEMORY OF THE

POET OF THE EAST

WHO SAID

ز خاک خویش طلب آتشے کہ پیدا نیست

تجلیے دگرے در خور تقاضا نیست

PREFACE TO THE SECOND EDITION

SINCE this book was first published Pakistan has come into being. In the creation of this State, many of the accepted conditions of nationhood like geographical cohesion and racial and linguistic affinities were subverted to the overriding unity of an ideal, that of practising the social values of Islam. The pursuit of this ideal brought success to this nation against overwhelming odds.

After the creation of the State the people were faced with many trials intrigued against us by our powerful enemies, but by the grace of Allah the State emerged stronger after every storm.

The ideal, however, which justified the creation of this State has yet to be translated into practice. Hesitation and timidity have marked the pace of the Government in this direction. This has been particularly so in the matter of interest, which still continues to govern all our financial relations. Even after making allowance for the difficulties which this Government had continually to face, and also the momentous nature of this problem, a start could certainly have been made by instituting a committee of experts to study the problem of interest and devise its substitute. To be remiss in this direction is to fail in the very purpose for which this country came into being.

In this edition discussion has been elaborated particularly in the chapters on Interest, Zakāt and Islamic Banking. The warmth with which the first edition has been received gives me the hope that these additions and the revision of the whole book will increase its utility.

Of late the problem of land reform has assumed great urgency. I had most unwillingly to content myself with a few passing references to this problem in the light of Islamic concepts. A full-dress discussion, I felt, would need greater space than what I could devote in a book of this type. I have therefore decided to treat this subject in a separate book[1], on which I am at present engaged.

If this book brings by even a day nearer the time when this country will bloom with the undying springs which the implementation of the social values of Islam can bestow on us, I shall have received the reward of my labour.

Mahmud Ahmad

Rawlakot
22 APRIL 1952

1. Since published by the Institute of Islamic Culture, entitled *Islam our Mas'ala-i-Zamin* (in Urdu).

PREFACE TO THE FIRST EDITION

The Scope of the Book. The Difference in Treatment from Other Works on the Subject. Justification for a Reference to Divine Sanctions.

The Scope of the Book

The book attempts to state clearly Islamic principles in the economic field. Derived as they are from the Qur'ān they have always been implicitly accepted by the Musalmans, even though they have not been always aware of the implications. They present the premises of an economic structure which, if worked out today, would be fundamentally different from the existing economic systems in the world. Besides stating those principles in detail, the book outlines the economic structure to which they logically lead. Leaving aside the Divine sanctions which they claim we need to examine them on purely rational grounds in order to bring out their bearing on the complex economic and social problems that face us today. An objective survey of the major economic systems, viz. capitalism, socialism and fascism, is made to bring out the bewildering problems that they present. In chapters devoted to Islamic economic principles, it is suggested how many of these problems are eliminated in the Islamic order. Our second inquiry has been to find out how far and in what way the economic order envisaged by Islam lends itself to be executed in practice under the modern circumstances. The Qur an prohibits interest in an exceptionally imperative tone. Is it possible to continue and extend healthy economic enterprise in the absence of interest? The answer to the question has been attempted in the chapter entitled Islamic Banking.

Generally, the effort has been not to trespass on domains which fall outside the scope of economics. The effort, however, has not always been successful. Social sciences, particularly economics and politics, are found at times, too closely linked to permit an exclusive treatment. Should an economic system lead to a peculiar political order, the evaluation of the former would be unbalanced without a reference to the latter.

The difference in Treatment from Other Works on the Subject

The books hitherto written on the subject do not present it scientifically. Generally, they are content to invoke the Divine sanctions for their principles. They forget that if Islamic economic order is something which can and ought to be practised today by the Musalmans, it should recommend itself to the non-Muslims with almost equal force, because the problems that confront the world today in the economic sphere are the same for Musalmans as, for any other religious group. But they completely bypass those problems, not to speak of trying to solve them. Even within the strictly limited sphere of Islamic economic principles they have failed to explain how they propose to surmount the difficulties that would arise in their execution. How do they propose to make credit available for the multifarious economic needs of a modern community once they reject the present banking structure? Wherefrom would an Islamic State get credit for its capital expenditure in the absence of the inducement of interest? Wherefrom would come capital for commerce and industry? What is Islam's substitute for bills of exchange? Who would supply investment for cottage industries and agriculture? This book attempts to answer all these questions. It also suggests Islamic solution for the wider and more important social problems: How can the crises be avoided? How to remedy the scourge of unemployment? How to surmount "capitalistic sabotage" and dumping? How to overcome the problem of mass poverty? And, finally, how to build a social structure better than socialism and fascism which, although solve most of these latter problems, yet create a new and equally intolerable situation, viz. the absence of personal liberty?

Justification for a Reference to Divine Sanctions

In search of answers to these questions, why should we turn to Divine sanctions, it may be asked. There are two reasons. One is that economics, which could have guided us in these social problems, is itself in a hopelessly chaotic condition. The relevant economic principles which we had to apply to these problems themselves stand impeached. No less a person than Lord Keynes confesses, "The classical theorists [he includes orthodox economists who follow Marshall] resemble Euclidean geometers in a non-Euclidean world, who, discovering that in experience straight lines apparently parallel often meet, rebuke the lines for not keeping straight as they only remedy for the unfortunate collisions which are occurring. Yet, in truth, there is no remedy except to throw over the axiom of parallels and to work out a non-Euclidean geometry. Something similar is required today in economics."[1] In such a fluid situation, it is natural that the economists who make a departure from the orthodox principles in search of a more acceptable system come out with explanations which contradict one another. The divergent views held about crises are one instance. On no important issue do they reach an agreement. Yet the problems are pressing. They cannot be postponed. Here we reach the second argument. There is a book which four hundred million people[2] believe to be the final book of guidance for mankind. It enjoins certain principles for a healthy economic order. Interpreted in modern circumstances they promise to solve perplexing problems. Once properly interpreted four hundred million people would like to execute them. Out of it one hundred million people who live in India are keen to be the first to make the experiment.

---

1. J. M. Keynes, *The General Theory of Employment, Interest and Money*, p. 16.
2. For this statement, I rely on the statistics given by Dr Zaki Ali in his *Islam in the World*.

Why not provide them an opportunity? They believe they would be successful. If they are, and the author has no reason to think otherwise, they will be able to guide the whole world in building up a healthy economic order, at once socially progressive and politically democratic, in which *laissez-faire* and socialism will attain a happy synthesis in which capital will be controlled and yet man will be free.

In the end I have to express my gratitude to Maulana Abul Kalam Azad for the help he gave me to understand certain aspects of Zakāt.

I have also to thank my friends and colleagues, Professor Abdur Rashid of P.W. College, Jammu, Professor P.N. Dhar of Delhi University, and Professors Hassan Shah and Ghulam Muhammad of S.P. College, Srinagar, who read various portions of the manuscript with me and helped me to improve it.

MAHMUD AHMAD

Srinagar

December 1946

CONTENTS

CHAPTER ③

The Unsocial Socialism, 38 - 65

CHAPTER ④

Zakāt, 66 - 89

CHAPTER ⑤

The Fascist Fiasco, 90 - 112

Chapter 1

The Capitalistic Chaos

What is Capitalism? The Claims of Capitalism. Its Culmination, A Chaos. Crises. Capitalistic Sabotage. Dumpling. Money: the Master, Chaos in Thought.

What is Capitalism?

"**CAPITAL** may be most briefly described as wealth used in producing more wealth and capitalism is the system directing that process" is the definition of capitalism given by *Encyclopaedia Britannica*. The term is of socialistic origin. It gained currency towards the second half of the nineteenth century. It denotes the worldwide process of organising production or trade on individualistic basis. Men with the help of previously accumulated wealth, but more often utilising money borrowed on interest, seek profit and fortune for themselves by employing the mass of human labour for wages.

Individual enterprise is the breath of capitalism. It permits absolute freedom to choose any one of the thousands of openings for productive or commercial effort, to choose any site, to employ any quantity or quality of agents of production, to select any market for them, and tò choose any method to dispose them of. This element of capitalism has been sharply criticised by socialists and fascists from their respective angles. The socialists have been offended by the enormous exploitation that individualistic capitalism permits. The fascist gibe at its waste and lack of planning. The socialists and fascist experiments, however, reveal that both nationalisation and planning involve an enormous amount of human suppression.

The real weakness of the capitalist system has been pointed out by neither. Their emphasis on exploitation and the absence of planning has gone a long way towards the elimination of these two defects in the later forms of capitalism. New Deal and Beveridge Schemes are instances in point. Yet the basic defects of capitalism show no sign of being cured. The attack, therefore, was not directed at capitalism's vulnerable point.

The second fundamental of capitalism is the institution of interest. If individualism be its breath, interest is its life-blood. Man in the course of his passage through time needs newer and finer things, and more and more of them. His needs are multiplying. So are the possibilities for producers and traders. But every man who enters the economic arena must have capital with him. Production is not possible without it. Trade is rarely so. Productive intelligence and commercial capability do not, generally, go hand in hand with capital. Generally, men who have money do not know what to do with it. And those who know do not have it. Both sets of men need to help one another. This necessity has led in the past to the founding of banks with interest as their basis. Those who have money to invest deposit it in banks for a fixed rate of interest. The banks lend this money to the other set for a higher rate of interest. They in return employ it in production or commerce and get, generally, a higher profit than the rate of interest. Apparently, there is nothing wrong in the system, religion apart. And people know how to compromise their religion.

Without going deep into the matter, we can detect two flaws in the arrangement. One is the position of the investor. Why is he paid? We shall consider this point at some length in the next chapter. It is sufficient to note at this place that the investor is paid without his taking and *active* part in the process of production. The second defect is from the point of view of the debtor. The initiative, enterprise and the risk are his. The addition to the total value of goods in the country will be in direct proportion to his intelligence and efficiency. But he is obliged to work with the burden of the yoke of interest. Interest is fixed. The bank is indifferent as to what the debtor might actually earn. The bank would claim a fixed interest even if the margin of profit left over to the debtor is negligible, or even if the deduction of interest makes him stand to lose. The result is that the active agent of production is underpaid to overpay the inactive one. The arrangement is essentially unjust. It is from this angle that Islam challenges capitalism.

The Claims of Capitalism

Capitalism has offered no serious defence against the attack made by Islam. But against the other attacks it claims that it is still the best economic system. The claim is based on the plea that economic processes under capitalism are self-adjusting and lead to the maximum satisfaction of human wants. Even while men seek maximum profit for themselves, they increase the happiness of others. In search of the cheapest supply of raw material, they reach that market where the raw material is abundant and hence cheap. They produce the thing for which there is the greatest demand. Thus they gain profit even while they are satisfying urgent human needs Similarly, in search of markets for their products they reach the place where those products are most urgently needed. Every productive process provides more employment. It increases the nation's wealth. The increase in wealth creates new demands. To satisfying these demands a new productive process comes into being. "Every individual," wrote Adam Smith, "is continually exerting himself to find out the most advantageous employment for whatever capital he can command[1]. It is his own advantage and not that of the society which he has in view. But the study of his own advantage naturally, or rather necessarily, leads him to prefer that employment which is most advantageous to the society.....But directing that industry in such a manner as its produce may be of the greatest value, he intends only his own gain; and he is in this, as in many other cases, led by an invisible hand to promote an end which was no part of his intention. Nor is it always the worse for society that it was not part of it. By pursuing his own interest he frequently promotes that of the society more effectively than when he really intends to promote it."[1] About the middle of the nineteenth century the "invisible hand" was left out of economic considerations. Besides, by the end of the century, the defects of the capitalistic system had become too pronounced to permit early complacence. It was declared that checks were necessary to work the capitalist system to the best social advantage. A large body of economists, however, still maintain that the system should not be unduly interfered with; and that, left to work for itself with the minimum of control, it is still capable of providing the maximum happiness of the maximum number.

Its Culmination, A Chaos

The first shock to the capitalistic complacency came towards the latter half of the nineteenth century. The unorganised labourers were forced to work for long hours in the most unhygienic surroundings for a bare subsistence level. They had to handle hazardous machinery without any compensation for loss of life or limb. Slow deterioration of labourers' health was common, under-nourishment universal. The greedy capitalists did not stay at that. Women and children were employed in preference to men for even lesser wages. The more successful producers could now indulge in competition to knock out of market the small-scale producers. The remaining producers joined hands and formed trusts to enjoy the advantage of monopoly price. The result was that the national wealth was concentrating in fewer and fewer hands. Income-tax was on the increase, but so was destitution and disease. The widening gulf between the rich and the poor made the sensitive spirits of the age extremely critical of the situation. Dickens used both humour and pathos to depict the miserable conditions of the poor. In *Unto This Last*, *Ruskin* declared that it is welfare we need rather than wealth. Carlyle denounced vehemently the system which countenanced "cash payment" as "the sole nexus between man and man".[2] In spite of their

1. *Inquiry into the Nature and Causes of the Wealth of Nations*, Book Chapter 2.
2. Carlyle, Past and Present.

ignorance of economic principles which they betray in their criticism, one cannot but deeply respect the great humaneness of these Victorian prophets. His social conscience led Carlyle to make an observation which remains to this day a succinct statement of the chaos that is capitalism. "The manufacturers," he wrote, "groan for the two million shirts without available market, and the labourers for their two million backs uncovered."[3]

Much change has been effected in the capitalist world since the days of Carlyle. Factory legislation restricts the number of hours labourers can be made to work, prohibits the employment of women and children, provides sanitary surroundings for them and compensation in case of loss of life of limb. Simultaneously, the labourers have organised themselves into powerful unions and refuse to accept wages which are unreasonably low. Employment insurance schemes are run, not only by most of these unions, but also by some of the industrial countries like England. The labourer is not longer as helpless as he used to be. But the maladjustment pointed out by Carlyle persists. The system has shown itself incapable of liquidating unemployment except during wars. Never except during a global war has it been able to employ its productive resources to the full. And this when millions and millions of people are underfed and underclothed. Even with the partial employment of productive resources, the system suffers from chronic overproduction. "Always, even in the most prosperous times, there is a substantial amount of unemployment, and some capital resources are lying unused."[4] Again and again there are "two million shirts" for which there is no market, and "two million bare backs" for which there is no shirt!

Crises

In presenting a few chaotic phases of capitalism we shall first take the crises and the depression that follows them. Ever and again the capitalist world is faced with a sudden collapse. The producers realise suddenly that the goods they are engaged in producing will not be marketed. The financiers and the bankers

---

3. Ibid.
4. G.D.H. Cole, *The Intelligent Man's Guide Through World Chaos*, p. 160.

contract credit and even try to withdraw the existing advances. Many factories are stopped and unemployment increases. The existing factories reduce their output. The prices fall. The traders stop purchases anticipating further fall in prices. A further restriction of production results. The government's revenue contracts and they are forced to restrict expenditure providing social security just at the time when it is most needed. Thus millions of labourers are unemployed, thousands of factories are closed or underworked, though billions of people in the world need the good things of life which those factories and those labourers could have produced.

Almost every decade there comes a crisis generally followed by a slump. It stays for about three to five years. Slowly it gives way to a boom when most of the agents of production are employed once again. These slumps have given the greatest headache to the economists. They have hitherto failed to explain them to anybody's satisfaction, just as the business world has failed to overcome them. The explanations offered and the remedies suggested by them are an instance showing how orthodox economics and its present-day exponents fail to solve the major economic problems.

Let us hurriedly review the orthodox economists' explanations about slumps[5]. One school of economists considers the trade cycle to be an outcome of price movements which in turn depend upon the world supply of gold. This view was at one time widely held and still claims adherents,[6] but is not tenable. From the middle seventies to the middle nineties of the last century, the prices almost continuously fell, yet, taken as a whole, the period was of an exceptional advance in world prosperity. There were no doubt some oscillations too—the depressions of later seventies, middle eighties and early nineties—yet, on the whole the industrial advance was more rapid than even during the following twenty years! when the movement of prices was generally upward. Theoretically, there is nothing wrong with the

5. Readers not interested in a somewhat technical discussion may pass over the remaining portion of this section—Crises.

6. E.g. Professor Cassel, *Memorandum Presented to the Gold Delegation of the League of Nations.*

falling of prices because they can co-exist with prosperous conditions in commerce and industry.

Another school of economists observes that the change from prosperity to depression is invariably heralded by the contraction of credit. The central banks suddenly raise the rate of discount and bankers generally become very reluctant to make advances to the industrial world. They argue that if the bankers would go on lending so long as productive resources are available there would be no occasion for depression. But they forget that the bankers do not gain anything by contracting credit. They are forced by the objective condition obtaining in the business world to believe that further advances would be unsafe. They see that further advances would be employed in ventures that promise no profitable return. The objective phenomenon is there. The bankers only interpret that phenomenon and contract credit because they have reason to believe that further advances would not be safe.

Another explanation offered is that the causes of the trade cycle are mainly psychological. They try to show that the business world is subject to alternating fits of over-confidence and under-confidence. Confidence in any one industry tends to spread to the whole system and breeds further confidence. The herd-instinct of the business men makes them oblivious of certain errors of calculation, which, in a cooler atmosphere, they could have foreseen. When the original prospects in several ventures fail to be realised, business men shake off all confidence. Now pessimism spreads further pessimism till depression sets in. Here again they fail to see anything wrong in the objective situtation. Both confidence and pessimism are born of success or failure in the business world. They are the reflection of the objective phenomenon, not its originators. "It is highly paradoxical," as Professor Cole has pointed out, "to treat the mental reactions and not the objective facts which they reflect or distort as the underlying causes of industrial progress or recession."[7]

Another theory associated with the name of Mr. J. A. Hobson sees the clue in the widening gulf between profits and

7. G.D.H. Cole. op. cit., p. 333.

wages during prosperity. Profits have a tendency to rise and real wages, a tendency to fall during the boom. Profits are not consumed and are invested in productive instruments. But the decrease in real wages reduces the purchasing power of the people. Thus, further investments beyond a certain point are only heading for disaster since they will produce things which no one will have the power to purchase. Disparity between purchasing power and productive output has indeed much to do with slumps. But the theory fails to give the remedy. How can this disparity be removed?

This does not exhaust the list of theories about crises. Indeed, it would be futile to record them all in a book of this type. Particularly when we remember the story that ten economists questioned about any controversial subject would give ten explanations, but questioned about crises they will offer eleven! However, we shall examine at some length the theory propounded by Lord Keynes. He has examined more acutely than anyone else the fundamental defects in the premises of economic and capitalists structure which tend to bring chaos. The suggestions made by him take a direction which, stretched to their logical conclusions, approximate the Islamic economic structure.

He considers interest one of the basic determinants of the economic system.[8] A healthy economic system should seek the fullest utilisation of all the productive resources available. But the rate of interest on money is the chief obstacle in the way. "The money rate of interest," he writes, "by setting the pace for all the other commodity rates of interest, holds back investment in the production of these other commodities without being capable of stimulating investment for the production of money, which by hypothesis cannot be produced."[9]

The two other determinants of the system are the marginal efficiency of capital and the propensity to consume.[10] The marginal efficiency of capital itself is pulled down by the rate of interest. "If seems then," he writes, "that the rate of interest on

8. J.M. Keynes, *The General Theory of Employment, Interest and Money, p. 184.*
9. Ibid., p. 235.
10. Ibid., p. 184.

money plays a peculiar part in setting a limit to the level of employment, since it sets a standard to which the marginal efficiency of a capital asset must attain if it is to be newly produced.[11] So far as the propensity to consume is concerned, he is not sure of the effect that the rate of interest may have on it. He rejects the orthodox view that the propensity to consume fluctuates in the inverse ratio to the rate of interest. He, however, could have seen two ways in which rate of interest influences propensity to consume. Propensity to consume cannot exist in the absence of purchasing power. Purchasing power decreases with the reduction in employment. And employment is limited by the rate of interest according to his own theory. If the rate of interest could attract investment, it would ultimately increase purchasing power. But the rate of interest in many cases only increases savings. Liquidity preference restricts investment and encourages savings—savings employed in government loans or stock exchange operations or simply leaving money as deposits in banks. Thus, in this way also, interest encourages savings and counteracts propensity to consume. In this direction Keynes has not worked out the logical implications of his own theory.

According to him, the crises result from the brake that is put on the wheels of the economic machine by the rate of interest. "Interest both initiates and aggravates crises."[12] But, he adds that a sudden collapse in the marginal efficiency of capital is, nevertheless, the primary cause of it. According to his own showing, marginal efficiency of capital is limited by the rate of interest.[13] So that he should have seen that the primary and fundamental cause of crises lies in interest. This is another lapse in his otherwise brilliant exposition.

In spite of these failures in logical consistency, it is to be confessed that, through the confusion of conflicting conceptions and complexities of the capitalist world, Keynes has come nearest to building up a coherent and convincing theory. The crises which

---

11. Ibid., p. 222.
12. Ibid., p. 315.
13. Ibid., p. 222.

bring chaos in the capitalist world shall be avoided only if the capitalist world agrees to pull down the institution of interest.

Capitalistic Sabotage

Crises are by no means the only expression of capitalistic chaos. Far from it. Even during booms all is not well with the world. The first important thing about booms is that they are no booms at all. People too often forget that unemployment continues even during booms. Take, for instance, the year 1929. The boom was at its highest. The capitalist world was happy and certain about the future. But productive resources were not being employed to the full. Leaving aside the dumb-driven millions in Asia and Africa, even in the capitalist West there were millions of unemployed. The incomplete statistics available show that in the first quarter of 1929, there were 269,000 unemployed in Japan; 309,000 in Italy; 225,000 in Austria; 170,000 in Poland; 1,204,000 in Great Britain; 2,484,000 in Germany.[14] No boom, unless occasioned by a global war, has been able to eliminate unemployment. The structural impediments in capitalist machinery restrict its working at full speed at all times. We devote great attention to crises because during slumps the defects become more pronounced and the problems more pressing. But they exist all the time even during booms. The producers are always concerned with the maximum yield for themselves. They, therefore, are always on guard against producing things in any excess which might force them to reduce their prices. If the technicians were to have their way, they would flood the market with goods. But this is just what the producers cannot afford to permit. "It is their office to adjust supply to demand; that is to prevent unprofitable rate of output; that is to keep industrial efficiency 'sub-normal'; that is to practise "'capitalistic sabotage.'"[15] "Capitalistic sabotage" is one of the aptest phrases coined by Veblen. Millions need the good things of life that the factories can produce. But they are not produced because it does to suit the capitalist system to produce them.

---

14. Figures collected from various sources by G.D.H. Cole, op. cit., p. 312.
15. W. C. Mitchell, *What Velben Taught*, p. xliv.

Dumping

But the most inhuman aspect of the capitalist system is the destruction of goods after they have been produced. Gunther, in his *Inside Latin America,* gives the story of Brazil coffee which would be comic but for the tragedy of it. One of the greatest difficulties which Brazil faced was how to destroy its enormous crop of coffee!

At first in 1914, thinking of ways to get rid of it, the authorities decided on burial. Then they found that four million sacks (132 pounds each) take a lot of room, and that it was necessary to plough up an area practically of the size of Rhode Island. They found, secondly, that the coffee did not have any fertilizer value; it would not turn into nitrogenous products; in fact—on the contrary—it destroyed the soil!

The experts put their heads to together in consternation. They decided instead of burying the wretched stuff to throw it over-board. Thousands upon thousands of sacks were piled on barges at Santoo, hauled out to sea, and tossed into the water. What happened was that the coffee killed the fish and polluted the beaches for miles around.

So earth and water having failed, Brazil turned to fire. More complications; Coffee consists 11 per cent of water; and it won't burn. That is, it won't burn unless artificial fuel is used. So the authorities had to import kerosene—which is expensive—to help the flames along. It is calculated that it costs *1s. ½d.* a bag to burn the coffee; in shipping, warehousing, labour and fuel; quite aside from the price of the wasted coffee itself. So Brazil pays about £200,000 a year to *get rid* of its 4 million sacks surplus crop.[16]

The author of the *Grapes of Wrath* depicts the unemployed in America going to seek employment in the orchards and farms of California. Because too many had come to seek employment, the wages came down to bare subsistence level. Even at that the great majority of newcomers were left unemployed. This underfed mass of mankind fell an easy prey to disease, and death. Even when they were dying in their hundreds, the orchards produced enormous quantities of fruit. According to the calculations of the proprietors, a major portion of the produce needed to be destroyed. Cherries and strawberries were left rotting on the trees while thousands begged to be allowed to gather them for just one meal as wages. But the proprietors could not agree. Then came

---

16. John Gunther, *Inside Latin America*, p. 315.

the oranges. They were gathered. The proprietors calculated. If the whole crop be put in the market, the prices would fall. A good portion must, therefore, be destroyed. The delicious oranges were gathered in the form of a golden mountain.. Petrol was sprayed over it and the mountain was burnt to ashes. This was done when in the same California children were dying because they were under-nourished.

During the last slump, a systematic destruction of things was going ahead. Agricultural Adjustment Administration in America has the following achievement to its credit.[17]

Allocation	*Approximate sum*
Cotton acreage ploughed up	*$ 110 million*
1934 cotton acreage reduction	*$ 150 million*
Emergency pig-sow slaughter	*$ 33 million*
Corn-hog production control	*$ 350 million*
Wheat acreage reduction	*$ 102 million*
Tobacco acreage reduction	*$ 21 million*

"In 1934, a million oranges were dumped into the sea in Liverpool harbour, to prevent the supply lowering the price of orange in the market—orange which to the children of the Liverpool poor is an unobtainable luxury. Nearer home one finds orders being issued for the restriction of 121 million pounds of tea in India, Ceylon and the Dutch Indies."[18]

The facts are too eloquent to need a comment.

Money: the Master

One of the most intelligent of men who spent a lifetime in pondering over the problems which the capitalist world presents was Thorstein Veblen. He explained that money, besides being a means of exchange, shapes our habits and thoughts. "Instead of being a machine for doing quickly and commodiously what would be done, though less quickly and commodiously, without it, the use of money exerts a distinct and independent influence of its

17. Figures taken from R.P. Dutt, *Fascism and Social Revolution*, p.45. quoting from *The Economist*, 30 Dec. 1933.
18. Hirendra Nath Mukerjee, *An Introduction to Socialism*, p. 16.

own upon our wants as consumers, upon our skill as planners, upon our methods as producers and upon our ideals as citizens."[19]

He explained this strange behaviour of money in his *Theory of the Leisure Class*. He argued that when success is measured in terms of money, "our native propensity towards emulation takes on a pecuniary twist". We cultivate the manners of the rich. We try to indulge in social frivolities and keep up with the changing styles. We practise "conspicuous leisure," and get satisfaction from "conspicuous waste". Money so permeates our culture that our sense of beauty comes to be stamped with the dollar sign. The costlier a thing is, the handsome it looks. That there is some structural flaw in the capitalist order which makes money influence our culture and habits of thought, is certain. The result of this influence is that money which was instituted to facilitate exchange has become our master It worked for us no doubt. But we also work for it. In fact, we go on working for it even when we not longer need it. Money in the capitalist system subjugates man. His success comes to be measured in terms of possession of money rather than creation. That is why Veblen challenged the orthodox economists who maintain that Marginal Utility Theory applies in the case of money. Money may have had marginal utility if it were only used to satisfy everyday human wants.

But money is also needed to establish our success in life. There is no marginal utility for success. And since success is measured in terms of money there is no marginal utility for money either.

Chaos in Thought

That the present capitalist structure is a chaos would be obvious to all unprejudiced readers by now. Improvement could be effected if men could be convinced that there is something wrong in the capitalistic world in which they live. They could then start analysing and arrive at the fundamental defect which lands us in this confusion of inhuman poverty in the midst of enormous productive resources which men could employ if they were free from the bondage of money.

---

19. W.C. Mitchell, op cit., pp, xxxix-xl.

This confusion becomes worse confounded when economists themselves fail to reach any agreement about any of the controversial subjects. Many hope that things would work out for the good in the end. In the meantime most of the economists remain wedded to the orthodox economic theories which stand impeached in the existing state of affairs. A few, like Keynes, have realised that there is some structural defect in the economic theory. "If orthodox economics is at fault," he confesses, "the error is to be found not in the superstructure, which has been erected with great care for logical consistency, but in a lack of clearness and of generality in the premises".[20] But his fellow economists wedded to orthodoxy would refuse to admit it. Meanwhile their important conceptions which could help in resolving the capitalistic conflicts themselves stand contradicted by the chaotic situation that they bring about. The theory of employment and interest has been irrefutably rejected by Keynes. Veblen has shown how Marginal Utility Theory applied to money is untenable. We are indeed in deep water. "The wild duck has dived down to the bottom—as deep as she can get—and bitten fast hold of the weed and tangle and all the rubbish that is down there, and it would need an extraordinarily clever dog to dive after and fish her up again."

20. J.M. Keynes, op. cit., p.v.

Chapter 2

Interest

The Qur'ān's Injunctions about Interest. What is Interest? What is not Interest? Interest. Venom for any Economic Order. Why should Interest be paid? Interest and Crises. Interest and "Capitalistic Sabotage." Interest and Dumping Interest and Culture. Interest or Profit.

The Qur'ān's Injunctions about Interest

ISLAM'S attitude to interest is clear and unambiguous. The relevant verses of the Qur'ān leave us in no doubt about it. But the average Musalman, sandwiched as he is between the colossal ignorance of our religious leaders and bewildering economic problems of the world, has very often lost his hold on Islamic principles as well as their economic implications. Let us read once against what the Qur'ān (Sūrah ii.) says about the matter:

274. Those who (in charity)
Spend of their goods
By night and by day,
In secret and in public,
Have their reward
With their Lord:
On them shall be no fear,
Nor shall they grieve.
275. Those who devour usury
Will not stand except
As stands one whom

The Evil One by his touch
Hath driven to madness.
That is because they say:
"Trade is like Usury,"
But God hath permitted trade
And forbidden usury.
Those who after receiving
Direction from their Lord,
Desist, shall be pardoned
For the past; their case
Is for God (to judge);
But those who repeat
(The offence) are companions
Of the Fire: they will
Abide therein (for ever).

276. God will deprive usury
Of all blessing,
But will give increase
For deeds of charity:
For He loveth not
Creatures ungrateful
And wicked.

277. Those who believe
And do deeds of righteousness,
And establish regular prayer
And regular charity
Will have their reward
With their Lord:
On them shall be no fear
Nor shall they grieve.

278. O ye who believe!
Fear God, and give up
What remains of your demand
For usury, if ye are
Indeed believers.

279. If ye do it not,
Take notice of war
From God and His Apostle:
But if ye turn back,
Ye shall have
Your capital sums:
Deal not unjustly
And ye shall not
Be dealth with unjustly.

What does this word "usury" mean? The original word which is translated here as usury is *ribā*. *Ribā* literally means an excess or addition.[1] With reference to debts, it means any excess above the principal lent. Therefore, it includes both interest and usury. In fact, argument is superfluous in the presence of these clear verses. Verse 278 says discard usury (*lit.* excess); verse 279 says you can take back the capital sum. So what we are prohibited from taking is the excess over the capital sum. Since interest is also an excess over the capital lent, according to the Qur'ān, it is prohibited.

What is Interest?

If people had not indulged in wishful interpretation of these verses of the Qur'ān, it should have been unnecessary for us to consider further what is that excess, usury or interest, which the Qur'an so forcefully prohibits. But, unfortunately, people have too often let their fancy play a leading part in the interpretation of these verses. It has been particularly so since the advent of the industrial revolution when capital came to play a leading role in the industrial and commercial fields. Intelligent Musalmans in the nineteenth century saw on the one side the long strides that the West, helped by its banking structure, was taking in the domains of industry and commerce, and on the other the ignorance and lethargy of Musalmans dragging them rung by rung down the ladder of prosperity. They saw that banks were an indispensable equipment in the industrial and commercial mechanism. Musalmans could not advance without commerce and industry. Commerce and industry could not advance without banking. Therefore Musalmans should no longer shun interest, the basis of banking. But what about the Qur'ān which prohibits interest? It was with this line of argument that Sir Sayyid and men of his school approached the Qur'ān. They, therefore, translated the word *ribā* as usury and proceeded to differentiate it from interest. Usury, they said, refers to the primitive form of money-lending when money was advanced for consumptional purposes. It is indeed cruel, they said, that money advanced to men who need it for their day-to-day expenses should be made a basis of profit.

---

1. C.f. *Tāj-ul-'Urūs*: *Mufradāt* of Imam Rāghib; E.W. Lane, *Arabic-English Lexicon*.

And the Qur'ān did well to prohibit usury. Interest, on the other hand, is a reasonable charge for the use of money employed in productive processes—industry or trade. The borrower uses the money and gets some profit. It is reasonable for him to pay some interest to the lender whose advance enabled him to make that profit. They concluded that interest, therefore, is not prohibited by the Qur'ān.

But they forget several things which repudiate their argument. Even in the days of the Prophet the Jews of Median advanced money not only for consumptional purposes but also for trade. Similarly, modern banks advance money not only for productive purposes but also for consumptional purposes. In fact, the essential difference between primitive and modern banking is one of degree and development, not of kind. The most important thing is that this bearing of banking on commerce was known to the Arabs even during the Prophet's days. Indeed, it greatly surprised them that the Qur'ān should permit trade and prohibit interest; but the Qur'ān, in spite of knowing the strength of their argument—and let us add that of Sir Sayyid and men of his school—repeated: Yes, trade is permitted and interest is prohibited. Let us read the relevant verse again:

> Those who devour usury
> Will not stand except
> As stands one whom
> The Evil One by his touch
> Hath driven to madness.
> That is because they say:
> "Trade is like Usury."
> But God hath permitted trade
> And forbidden usury.[2]

Mark the last four lines. The Qur'ān foresees the bearing of interest on trade. Yet in its own glorious way it insists on permitting trade and prohibiting interest. So far as the alleged difference between usury and interest is concerned, there is nothing in the verses of the Qur'ān to justify it. As already pointed

2. ii. 275.

out, the word in the original is *ribā* which means excess or addition and therefore it covers both interest and usury.

It is indeed futile to say anything against Sir Sayyid. His sincerity cannot be questioned. He was a product of his age. Musalmans were suffering from an acute inferiority complex. And the West was advancing, conquering, displaying signs of a superior civilisation all around. The one remedy which occurred to him was to ask the Mussalmans to follow the West. But now the position has greatly changed. A renaissance has come to Muslim lands. Afghanistan, Iran, Iraq and Egypt have wrested independence from the foreign masters. So have Lebanon and Syria. Arabia has built up a stable Government. Turkey, the sick man of Europe, is a healthy little republic. The Muslims of Indonesia are asserting themselves in an unmistakable manner. Pakistan has come into being and avowedly affirms the social values of Islam as a means of building up a social democracy, free from the cramping material concepts of capitalism and communism. This urge for independence and self-expression has spread East and West, from the Pacific to the Atlantic. From Malaya to Morocco a conflagration has spread which will not rest till chains and gyves of bondage have melted. The West on the other hand repeatedly prepares for war as it cannot conquer peace. Its economic structure is vitiated by the running cancer of interest which lies in its womb. Having lost its spiritual mooring it is hastening to commit a *hara kiri* in a hail of H. Bombs. This decaying West now faces a renaissant Islam.

This entire argument was necessary because there are still those who have retained their pre-renaissance inferiority complex and are led to believe that the Qur'ān does not prohibit interest. Let us quote one of them:

> Our 'Ulamā', ancient and modern, have worked out a body of literature on usury, based mainly on economic conditions as they existed at the rise of Islam. I agree with them on the main principles, but respectfully differ from them on the definition of usury. As this subject is highly controversial, I shall discuss it, not in this commentary, but on a suitable occasion elsewhere. The definition I would accept would be: Undue profit made, not in the way of legitimate trade, out of loans of gold and silver, and necessary articles of food, such as wheat, barley, dates, and salt (according to the list

mentioned by the Holy Apostle himself). My definition would include profiteering of all kinds, but exclude economic credit, the creature of modern banking and finance.

It is indeed correct that the all-embracing word *ribā* (i.e. excess or addition) is capable of including profiteering. But why should the learned translator consider interest-bearing loans of gold and silver objectionable and bless currency loans, "the creature of modern banking and finance," passes one's comprehension. What difference is there, moral or technical, between a gold loan and a currency loan? Before the institution of paper money, gold, at first unminted and later on minted, was the medium of exchange and the measure and store of value. The same important functions are now performed by paper money backed by bank or State credit plus a certain percentage of paper money kept as gold reserve. In primitive days, loans were advanced in the form of precious metals or coins made therefrom; now loans are advanced in the form of cheques or notes. The Qur'ān is not concerned with the shape of our loans. It is concerned only with the "excess" —call it interest or usury or what you like—that we may charge or pay for the use of a loan. If we do not abstain, we are free to "take notice of war from God and His Apostle" (ii. 279)

It is, indeed, the same old habit of teaching the Qur'ān a little economics. They should have presumed that God knew a little more of it. What they should have said was: Of course the Qur'ān prohibits all forms of interest, but the Qur'ān is an obsolete book incapable of satisfying modern requirements. That would have been a more straightforward statement. If they said that, one could have referred them to the man who understood money and interest more than anyone else in this century. This is what Lord Keynes writes:

> There remains an allied, but distinct, matter where, for centuries, indeed for several millenniums enlightened opinion held for certain and obvious a doctrine which the classical school[3] has repudiated as childish, but which deserves rehabilitation and honour. I mean the doctrine that the rate of interest is not self-adjusting at a level best suited to the social advantage but constantly tends to rise too high, so

---

3 Keynes includes Marshall and his followers in the classicial school. *The General Theory of Employment, Interest and Money*, p. 3.

that a wise government is concerned to curb it by statute and custom and even by invoking the sanctions of the moral law[4].

What havoc is wrought by interest, we shall see in a minute. But first let us be clearer as to what the Qur'ān means by "excess" or interest.

What is not Interest?

If we start from the negative end, the Qur'ān's meanings become obvious. The clue is provided by verse 275 of Chapter ii:

> They say
> "Trade is like Usury,"
> But God hath permitted trade
> And forbidden usury.

Why does God permit trade and forbid usury? Capital invested in trade brings an excess called profit, invested in banking it brings interest. God prohibits one excess and permits another. What is the difference between the two? The difference is that profits are the result of initiative, enterprise and efficiency. They result after a definite value-creating process. Not so with interest. It may even retard a value-reciting or productive process and too often does, as we shall soon seen. A still more fundamental difference is that interest is fixed, profit fluctuates. In the case of interest you know your return and can be sure of it. In the case of profit you have to work to ensure it. If a banking structure could be evolved in which the return for the use of money would fluctuate according to the actual profits made from it, Islam would have no objection to it. That would be a developed from of *shirākat* which is already recognized in Islamic jurisprudence. What the Qur'ān prohibits is a fixed return for the use of money irrespective of the profit gained or the loss incurred by the borrower. So *ribā* or interest means: *Fixed return for the use of money*. It is always prohibited whether it results from the "loans of gold and silver" or "economic credit, the creature of modern banking and finance".

Against this set of people who have sought to exclude "economic credit" from the Islamic conception of interest, there is

---

4. Ibid.

a critic of Islam who includes even land rent in interest. Professor Smith writes:

> It is hardly necessary to add that these religious proponents not only have never put forward the argument, but cannot even understand, that the prohibition of interest, if taken seriously, would include the prohibition of land rent and of the whole landlord system—would mean precisely the socialization of agriculture in the interests of those who labour on land.[5]

By what stretch of argument the author includes land rent in interest, he has not explained. The present writer had an interview with Professor Smith and asked him to elucidate this point. He said that, although, technically, they are different, morally they are identical. Of course, where tenants are made to pay a fixed rent whether in cash or in kind, it is morally identical with interest. Because, here, the landlord is to the same extent indifferent to the actual return from land as the banker is to the actual return from industry or commerce. But all land rent is not of this type. By far, the major part of land rent in Muslim India is got by what is called *batā'i* system. The landlord and the tenant share the yield of land generally in the proportion of fifty-fifty. This *bata'i* rent has got nothing to do with interest. This, however, does not amount to say that all is well with the landlord system. The system of *batā'i* has been sealing the productive urge of the tenants and depriving them of the fruits of their labour. It has outlived its utility when a strong man used to give protection to tenants, their properties and produce and took a share of the harvest. Now no depradator threatens the tenant and the landlord performs no function which may entitle him to a share of the produce of land. There is nothing in Islam to prevent us from abolishing this. Unlike socialism, Islam does not permit appropriation of lands without compensation. The landlord should be paid out at a multiple of their annual income which the tenants should pay in instalments spread over a number of years. At the end the tenants should become the owners of land. It will be the practical interpretation, in the context of today, of that saying of the Holy Prophet: "The land belongs to the one who quickens the dead earth of life."

---

5. Wilfred Cantwell Smith, *Modern Islam in India*, p. 107.

Interest, Venom for any Economic Order

Locke quotes from *A Letter to a Friend Concerning Usury:* "High interest decays trade. The advantage from interest is greater than the profit from trade, which makes the rich merchants give over, and put out their stock to interest, and the lesser merchants break."[6] Since the days so Locke, the process in which interest decays trade and industry has become a little complex. But its negative effect still remains. The only difference is that now interest does —or undoes— the job without needing the epithet high.

Economists have justified interest on the assumption that capital is an important agent of production. The justification would have been valid if interest was related to the actual proceeds from the process of production. But interest is not. Capital charges a fixed return irrespective of what the actual income may be. The result is that it weighs down and retards the growth of the productive process. Capital itself is an agent of production. But interest on capital undoes its productivity. Interest, to but it in scientific language, sets a limit to the marginal efficiency of capital. When the marginal efficiency of capital is reduced, it leaves several productive resources unemployed. Two results follow. On the one hand, the limited use of the productive resources reduces the amount of goods produced. On account of the charge of interest, their marginal cost of production rises. So that they have to be sold at a higher price. On the other hand, much labour is left unemployed. So that the economic system based on interest always runs the risk of manufacturers groaning for their "two million shirts unsold" and labourers for their "two million backs uncovered". How much difference would it have made if there were no interest. The "two million shirts" could have been sold cheaper because of the reduction in their cost of production. On the other side, the two million labourers could have found employment if the brake on the marginal efficiency of capital were removed. More purchasing power on the one hand and lower prices on the other would have

6. Quoted from J.M. Keynes, op. cit., p. 344.

helped to cover the "two million bare backs" with the "two million shirts" which in interest - ridden economy find no market.

Interest, however, works in a more complex manner to vitiate our economy. For people who have money to save and invest, it provides a liquid form of investment. Their spare money is gravitated to banks where they are assured a fixed percentage of interest without taking any part in the productive process. The economists have presumed that the money so gravitated would be employed in industry and commerce. But in practice the presumption is rebutted. Quite a substantial part of banks' assets is diverted to unproductive channels. Banks invest in government securities, advance money for speculative purposes, and cash bills of exchange. None of these is a productive process. Not even the bills of exchange. Although they facilitate trade, interest on them increases still further the price of goods. In an ideal economic system, bills of exchange should be cashed free, and we shall see in the chapter on Islamic Banking how this can be done. Here the point is that the institution of interest provides banks with unproductive channels to employ their capital. So that capital which should have been available for productive purposes becomes scarce. Simultaneously, the institution of banks tends to preclude people from investing their money directly in industry and commerce. This produces scarcity of capital available for productive purposes. The scarcity of capital raises the rate of interest. The increase in the rate of interest only accentuates the vicious influence of interest. More purchasing power diverted to banks; more banks' assets diverted to liquid and unproductive channels; a further reduction in the marginal efficiency of capital; a further limitation of employment; a further rise in the price of goods, and lastly a further spectacle of "two million shirts" without market and "two million backs uncovered".

If there were no interest, the result would be that the purchasing power of the people would be either used in satisfying their desires or invested in industries or commerce either directly or through banks based on the principle of sharing the actual return from investments. The portion of purchasing power people would spend on their immediate needs which would create a demand for goods which would encourage production. The portion they would invest in commerce or industry would provide capital for further productive processes. Either way production would be spurred and employment provided. But the depositor in banks neither invests nor spends. He simply hoards. Banking is really a highly developed form of hoarding. The difference between primitive hoarding and present banking is this: When people burried their store of value under the earth their treasures ran the risk of deterioration and loss. Not so in modern banking. There is no risk in a good bank; and the value seldom decreases. The second difference is that the depositor in a bank goes on getting interest even though his money may not be employed in any productive process. This advantage was absent in primitive hoarding. The result is that from the social point of view modern banking is worse than primitive hoarding. We never rewarded the hoarders in the past. But we reward the modern depositor with a fixed rate of interest. So that the people who do the most unsocial of works, viz. the depositors and the bankers, are the only people who go on amassing wealth. They cause the mass of men to suffer in grinding poverty. Here someone may object that the banks do not invest all their resources in unproductive jobs like government securities, loans for speculative and consumptional purposes and bills of exchange. The answer is that when banks do grant long-term industrial loans—although, generally, they are very reluctant to do it—they limit the marginal efficiency of the capital they advance by the interest that they charge on it. We have already seen to what this limitation of marginal efficiency leads: To "two million shirts" without available market and "two million backs uncovered".

Why Should Interest be Paid?

Let us see the various theories that have been hitherto advanced for the payment of interest. All the great ancient thinkers regarded the payment of interest unjust. Aristotle condemned it because a piece of money could not beget another.[7] Plato, too, was opposed to it.[8]

In the Middle Ages the Christian Church was against the payment of interest and charging of usury was prohibited by Common Laws. The latter economists have all along regarded this prohibition as a mere dogma, which was blind to the working and value of capital. Keynes, however, feels differently about this: "It now seems clear that the disquisitions of the Schoolmen were directed towards the elucidation of a formula which could allow schedule of the marginal efficiency of capital to be high, while using rule and custom and the moral law to keep down the rate of interest."[9]

The early mercantilists advocated a low rate of interest. These included Sir Thomas Culpeper and Sir Josiah Child. There were others like Mun and Thomas Manley who contended that to lower the rate of interest either the supply of money should increase of the demand for money should decrease. To refer to demand and supply might show *how* interest is determined, but does not answer the question why is it paid at all.

Nassu William Senior regarded interest as a price paid for abstinence, or postponing consumption. This came to be called as the Abstinence Theory of Interest. He was very suitably served by the socialist writer Lasalle: "The profit of capital is the 'wage of abstinence'. Happy, even priceless expression. The ascetic millionaires of Europe, like Indian penitents or pillar saints, stand on one leg each on his column, with straining arm and pendulous body and pallied looks, holding a plate towards the people to collect the wages of their abstinence. In their midst, towering up above all his fellows, as head penitent and ascetic, the Baron Rothschild."[10]

Later on Marshall, to avoid this objection, used the world "waiting" for abstinence. But will this withered rose called by another name smell sweeter? Waiting is not by itself a productive

---

7. Aristotle, *Politics*, Book I. Chapter X.
8. Plato, *Laws*, Book V.
9. J.M. Keynes. op. cit., p. 352.
10. Quoted by Bohm-Bawerk, *Capital and Interest.*

act. Savings may be hoarded or directed in unproductive channels and yet interest may be paid for them. It provides no justification for interest.

Adam Smith and Richardo, the founders of the classical school, regarded interest as the compensation which the borrower paid to the lender for the profit the former would make by the use of the latter's money. Ricardo observes, "Whenever a great deal can be made by the use of it, a great deal can be given for the use of it."[11] This only means that the lender deserves to share the profits that the borrower may make. How to relate these profits that are variable to interest that is fixed, is nowhere shown. Neither these, nor any other economist, appear to face, much less answer, this basic question on the Productivity Theory of Interest.

Another argument given by Smith and Ricardo is that interest is an inducement for savings. How would they have explained the enormous increase in savings during this century along with a steep fall in the rate of interest? Savings do not so much depend on interest as on the level of investment and employment in a society. "The initiative," writes Joan Robinson, "lies with the entrepreneurs and not with the savers. The savers, as a group, are helpless in the hands of entrepreneurs, though any one individually is free to save as much as he likes."[12]

If we leave out of consideration, as we must, the Abstinence Theory, as having failed to justify interest, we are only left with the Productivity Theory which makes that claim. The advocates of this theory regard productivity as an inherent property of capital and justify interest as a reward for this productivity. While no one can deny the productivity of capital, its reward should be related to the actual contribution made by capital to the productive process. We cannot assume expectations and actualities to be identical, as this theory does, since in practice they seldom are. All productive theories of interest, including the most accepted version, the Marginal Productivity Theory of Interest, lack dimension. They treat the economic system as something static, whereas it is essentially mobile. Every moment

11. Ricardo, *Principles of Poltical Economy and Taxation.*
12. Joan Robinson, *Introduction to the Theory of Employment, p. 13.*

it seeks a new equilibrium, with changes in tastes, populations, standards of living, values and quantities of currencies, savings, investments and inventions. All these changes act and react on each other and cumulatively affect the value of each unit of capital that may be employed. To disregard all this mobility which influences the value of capital is being too naive.

The Austrian Theory of Interest is associated with the name of Bohm-Bawerk. "Present goods are," he writes, "as a rule, worth more than future goods of like kind and number. This proposition is the kernel and the centre of the interest theory which I am going to present."[13] He, therefore, concludes that a loan without interest is equivalent to a sale below market price. Even this proposition, this kernel and centre of the theory, disregards a fact of universal prevalence. In all countries and climes, wherever the men have the capacity to save, they do so for the rainy day, in total disregard of the premium or otherwise on savings. And when men cannot save, have barely enough to live on, no rate of interest can persuade them to starve. Here, of course, present goods are of much more value than future goods. But the men in this situation have no capacity to give loan and should as little enter the theories of interest as they do the money market. Those who can save, as a rule, do, sacrificing present comforts to future necessities. In their case, this Agio or Time-Preference Theory is as inapplicable as in the case of corporate savings, which form the bulk of savings in advanced countries, and which are made for the sake of security and financial stability of various concerns. Will these concerns become indifferent to their future stability if there be no interest? Obviously not.

Some of the followers of Bohm-Bawerk, like Kunt Wicksel and Von Hayek, emphasise the Marginal Productivity Theory of Interest; others like Fetter and Fisher stick to the Time-Preference Theory, both of which we have examined above and found most inadequate.

Indeed, all theories of interest fail to answer the simple question: Why should interest be paid? They either point to

---

13 Bohm-Bawerk, *Positive Theory of Capital* (Smart's translation), p. 251.

waiting or to productivity of capital or to both. But neither the one, nor the other nor both of them, are any answer to the objection: How can productivity of capital (which is variable) justify interest (which is fixed)?

The later-day theories of interest make no attempt to answer: Why interest is paid? They, instead, only explain how it is determined. It appears that economists, having groped for some time to discover a solid basis for the payment of interest, sought an easy escape for themselves in the theory of price: demand and supply which determine the price of all things determine the price of capital as well. They appear to have forgotten that the theory of price is a problem of Exchange, whereas the theory of interest is a problem of Distribution. This objection applies to all modern theories of interest. They are called monetary theories of interest because they take a note of the amount of money available in a period; they also relate interest to the instinct of hoarding as the Swedish school does, or to Liquidity Preference, which Keynes emphasises. According to the Loanable Fund Theory, "the rate of interest is the price that equates the supply of credit, or savings plus net increases in the amount of money in a period, to the demand of credit, or investment plus the net hoarding in the period,"[14] According to Keynes, the rate of interest is determined by the interplay of the terms on which the savers desire to become more or less liquid and those on which the banking system is ready to become more or less illiquid. Both these theories are essentially demand and supply theories of interest and do not provide any justification for the payment of interest. The various agents of production contribute to the creation of national wealth. Capital can draw its share from the increase of national wealth only to the extent of its contribution to it. Capital cannot be allowed to run away with its pound of flesh, determined in advance, and unrelated to the actualities of production. These theories of interest do not take note of the fact that the *fixity* of the rate of interest weighs down the elasticity of the processes of production. It retards their innate mobility and stultifies their

14. A P Leave, "Alternative Formulations of the Theory of Interest." *Economic Journal, 1938.*

growth. It is only the Islamic theory of capital profit that can meet all these objections. It states that capital will share the value produced by it, to be determined as a percentage of the profits earned rather than a percentage of the capital itself. The percentage of profits is a variable sum, and, therefore, does not impose any restraint on production. Unlike interest, it is responsive to the dynamic and mobile nature of production. All variable determinants of value, named and unnamed, including population, currency, tastes, habits, investments, inventions, savings, standards of living, and a host of others are included by its nature in the Islamic theory of capital profits, while all the Western theories of interest leave them out as we have seen above (except the Loanable Fund Theory which takes a note of changes in currency). But the Islamic theory takes a note of all variables by making the reward of capital variable, according to what achievement is made by capital. Insistence on fixed interest has confined and contradicted capitalism. Some of the ways in which this has been done are explained below.

Interest and Crises

We saw in the last chapter that the greatest problem in the capitalist economy is that of the crises. They represent accumulation of goods in the absence of purchasing power and the propensity to consume. They withhold production, contract credit and create unemployment.

Interest plays a peculiar part in bringing about the crises. The process in which interest exerts this influence may be classified into three phases: (a) the primary phase, (b) the intermediary phase and (c) the final phase.

In the primary phase, interest sows the seed for the crisis. It takes place in the heydays of a boom. Large amounts of money on interest are employed in productive processes. Due to the burden of interest the marginal cost of production no doubt rises, but as yet there is enough demand for goods and the producers feel highly optimistic about the future. As the demand for goods is great, the profits rise and are reinvested in industry of banks. The wages, however, always lag behind. Interest has a bearing on this lagging behind of wages because the entrepreneurs carrying the burden of interest, are very reluctant to increase wages. Besides, a large number of labourers remain unemployed even during the nascent boom. In the high marginal cost of production and in the lagging behind of wages are sown the seeds of the invisible yet inevitable crisis.

The great profits made in the primary phase create a great optimism in the business world. They do not look to the lagging wages nor to the rising costs but simply want to produce goods. The demand for capital increases and the rate of interest continues to rise. The business men with their short term vision go on attracting liabilities in spite of the rising costs of production. In this intermediary phase the demand for capital for speculative purposes also increases—again rising the rate of interest. The producers, however, continue to produce, although the margin to profit now starts contracting. Many producers see that in their over-confidence they have started ventures which do not promise to pay. The first signs of over-production become noticeable.

In the final phase the banks, seeing that further demand on capital would be used for purposes which promise no return, desire to contract credit. The central bank generally raises the signal by increasing the rate of discount. The banks raise their rate of interest to a prohibitive level. They even try to withdraw the former loans, thus increasing unemployment on the one side and raising an alarm in the business world on the other. Prospective purchasers now prefer to postpone purchases till prices fall. This produces lack of consumers. Lack of purchasers on the one side and withdrawal of loans on the other make many unstable structures fall. It is only when the accumulated goods are consumed–between three to five years determined by the carrying cost on the stock estimated by Keynes at 10%—that production starts over again.

The intermediary and the final phases have been explained well enough by W.C. Mitchell giving an account of Veblen's teachings:

When times are good, prices rise, profits are high, business men borrow freely and enlarge their output. But such prosperity works its own undoing. The substantial security behind the loans is prospective net earnings capitalized at the current rate of interest. When the rate of interest rises, as it does during prosperity, the capitalized value of a given net income declines, and the loans become less safe. More than that net earnings in many cases prove less than had been expected in the optimistic days of the nascent boom. Prices cannot be pushed up indefinitely: the costs of doing business rise and encroach upon profits: bank reserves fall and it becomes difficult to get additional credit. When fading profits are added to high interest, creditors become nervous. In such a strained situation, the embarrassment of a few conspicuous concerns will bring down the unstable structure which had seemed so imposing. A demand for liquidation starts and spreads rapidly, for the enterprises pressed for payment put pressure on their debtors to pay up. So prosperity ends in a crisis, followed by depression.[15]

But we have seen that before all this happens, even when there are no apparent signs of a crisis, the seed is sown in the high costs of production and the lagging behind of wages both in different measures contributed by interest.

In the above discussion, besides the bearing of interest on crises, we have seen that the business world works with a peculiar short-sighted vision. What is the reason? Banks have a bearing on this as well. The banks like to supply only short term credit. This short-term credit forces the producers to adopt this peculiar short-term policy. Due to short-term measures, they only increase the costs of goods they produce. For, instead of installing up-to-date devices, they only work obsolete machinery overtime. When the times are good, they naturally want to make the best of it. So long as there is a market, they go on producing; when the crisis is signalled by the rise in interest, they get the tip and contract production. In the entire process, the short-term credits force the producers to adopt a short-term policy and let the devil take care of the recurrent crises.

The abolition of interest can abolish the crises. Capital would not be a burden on the productive machine. Production would extend to that length which can provide employment to everybody. There is no technological reason, once the brake of interest is removed, to restrict production when millions of men in the world need the good things of life which the machines, human

---

15. W.C. Mitchell, *What Veblen Taught*, pp xliii-xliv.

skill and human labour are always willing to produce. It is the "enchantment" of interest that there are goods without market and men who need them but cannot purchase them. "Enchantment"[16] is the word which Carlyle used for this strange phenomenon. But God had promised it in the Holy Qur'ān:

> Those who devour usury
> Will not stand except
> As stands one whom
> The Evil One by his touch
> Hath driven to madness[17].

"The Evil One" has touched the entire West because they "devour usury" and has "driven it to madness". Mus̈almans planning for a healthy economic order would do well to heed the warning of the Qur'ān.

Here the reader might question: Agreed that interest is a poison seeping in the body of the capitalist system, but what other basis of credit can there be? We will examine this question in the chapter on Islamic Banking. Here we had only to show that the abolition of interest can cure the scourge of the crises bringing in their wake poverty and unemployment.

Interest and "Capitalistic Sabotage"

If the above discussion makes clear the bearing of interest on the crises, it should become equally clear that "capitalistic sabotage" will have no place in the Islamic economic system. "Capitalistic sabotage" is nothing but a form of depression. The business world, seeing a shortage in demand, restricts production. The goods are all the time needed by the world. In fact, the world can absorb all the goods that machinery can produce and much more. The absence of demand is due to the absence of purchasing power. With the abolition of interest, purchasing power would be increased because production could be extended without the restraint of interest. Simultaneously, there would be a reduction in the marginal cost of production of goods. The two things, cheaper

---

16. Carlyle, *Past and Present.*
17. ii. 275.

goods and more employment, would exclude all need of "capitalistic sabotage".

Interest and Dumping

The same argument holds good about dumping. This is indeed an inhuman system to destroy finished goods when millions in the world need them. But those who destroy them are forced to do it by the problem of demand and supply. The supply is great and if the whole thing be marketed, the price would possibly be lower than even the marginal cost of production. Again two things need to be done: (1)reduction in the marginal cost of production which would be obtained if there is no interest: (2) increase in the purchasing power of the masses. Abolition of interest will, again, play an important part in doing so. Because production gaining relief from the brake of interest would be able to extend in all directions providing employment to millions. Employment would increase purchasing power. Purchasing power would increase demand. Lower price resulting from a drecrease in the marginal cost of production would again whip up demand. So that the goods that now can serve no better purpose than being burnt or thrown into the sea will be available for millions who never had the good fortune to use them in their lives. Indeed, we are only "driven to madness" when we burn oranges or dump coffee. If we only avoid "the touch" of "the Evil One" by abolishing interest, we shall regain our sense.

Interest and Culture

We have seen in the last chapter that in the peculiar circumstances obtaining in the capitalist West, money has come to exercise influences which were altogether unforeseen at the time of its creation. Money was created to facilitate trade. Money does this job. But it does another which we never wanted it to do. It has mastered us. It has influenced our ways of thinking and our notions now carry a money mark. It has thus affected our culture.

We analyzed in the last chapter that this is a result of money and possession thereof having become synonymous with success. Islam as a culture-pattern cuts across this tendency of money to become the master of man. It proclaims, first of all, the sovereignty of God. Man can never have two sovereigns. For a people who serve God, money cannot assume the role of a master. The second culture postulate of Islam is the brotherhood of man. High and low, rich and poor, are equal in the eyes of God and, what is more important, in the eyes of Musalmans. Interest, on the other hand, negatives a culture of brotherhood. Interest means to take a reward for your surplus money irrespective of what the debtor might do with it. You refuse to share his profit and loss, but simply burden him with the yoke of interest. Human brotherhood and sympathy evaporate when interest is charged for loans of money. But interest does more. It concentrates more and more money in the hands of those who lend, and does not increase the prosperity of those who take loans. The result is that a people who accept interests as the basis of their economic system come to have two classes: enormously rich who lend and enormously poor who cannot afford even the immediate necessities of life. The enormously rich can indulge in "conspicuous waste" and "conspicuous leisure". They are tempted to parade their success in life.

When this happens success comes to be measured in terms of money. Money then assumes the role of the master. But Islam excludes this possibility by the abolition of interest. Islam further taxes the enormously rich, and makes it incumbent on the Sate to provide for the poor. But we are anticipating the subject of another chapter. Here the point is that interest negatives both the sovereignty of God and the brotherhood of man and creates a possessing class which need not work, but still be sure of decent income for acting as parasites. Interest, though the creation of this class, adversely affects human culture and makes man subservient to money.

Interest or Profit

Many economists and other intelligent men have been convinced that there is something wrong with the capitalist structure. But, strange as it may seem, they lay stress on the wrong point and let go the banker free. They continue to believe that the banks provide life-blood to industry, even though poison be seeping in along with that blood. This wrong emphasis to a large extent is caused by the Marxian analysis. Marx had found profit motive to be the root cause of poverty and unemployment. He was a single track thinker who made up for the defects in argument in superb demagoguy. His Dialectical Materialism is made up of philosophy and history, economics and prophesies. But boiled down to a basic essential in economic terms, he opposed the profit motive. He sought the remedy in abolishing profit motive and communalising all instruments of production. He failed to see that the basic fault with the present economic order is not profit but interest. Profit is the whip for efficiency. It is the entrepreneur who brings together the different agents of production in proper proportions. It is his efficiency, enterprise and skill which guarantee the most efficient working of the productive process. Although in practice Russia has been forced to return to the introduction of profit motive, represented in piece-wages and the Stakhnovite movement, yet there are some economists with a socialist leaning who consider profit motive the source of all economic maladies. This is what G.D.H. Cole writes:

> But always, even in the most prosperous times, there is a substantial amount of unemployment, and some capital resources are lying unused.
>
> Why does this happen? Because those who control the existing capital resources and the means of making new ones do not see their way to using such resources to the full under conditions which will permit them to make a worthwhile profit by their use. They accordingly leave capital resources or the means of making them unused; and unemployed labour follows as a result of this abstention.[18]

The argument, so far as it goes, is sound. But it does not go far. The real question is: Why don't the people find any profit in employing their capital resources? Because their capital resources carry the burden of interest. Interest works in two directions with respect to capital resources. On the one side, it applies a brake on extending production. On the other, the banks attract capital which, otherwise, would have been used in extending production. The banks in their turn direct the capital in all sorts of unproductive channels: government securities, bills of exchange,

---

18. G.D.H. Cole, *The Intelligent Man's Guide Through World Chaos*, p.160.

speculation and consumptional loans. Remove this brake of interest and people in possession of capital resources will find it profitable to employ them. In fact, that will have no other profitable avenue left with them like the present-day banks. Indeed, it is surprising that intelligent men like Professor Cole should denounce profit, the guarantee of all efficiency; and say not a word against interest, particularly when he is ware of the unproductive nature of finance. This is what he writes:

> Finance by itself produces nothing; and money is of value only for the buying of things. It is therefore plainly wrong for monetary conditions to govern industry, or for production to be made the handmaid of finance.[19]

Indeed, it is plainly wrong. But the plain remedy for this plain wrong is to abolish interest. For, it is interest that enables finance to govern production. The remedy does not lie in abolishing the profit motive. That would be like throwing away the baby instead of the bath-water. It is because profit is the guarantee of efficiency and interest the canker-worm that:

> God hath permitted trade
> And forbidden usury.[20]

19. Ibid., p. 297.
20. The Qur'ān, ii. 275.

Chapter 3

The Unsocial Socialism

What is Socialism? Marx, the Philosopher, Marx, the Historian. Marx, the Economist. Marx the Prophet. The Problem of Efficiency, Is Marxism Dead? Achievements of Socialism. The Price of Socialism. The Unsocial Socialism.

What is Socialism?

"Socialism is essentially a doctrine and a movement aiming at the collective organisation of the community in the interests of the mass of the people by means of the common ownership and collective control of the means of production and exchange."[1] Socialism has drawn its strength from the desire of sensitive men in all ages from Plato's *Republic* to Ruskin's *Unto This Last* to seek a more equitable distribution of the means of livelihood. It was about 1830 that the word "socialism" first came to be used simultaneously in England and France. It was employed in England to describe the teachings of Robert Owen with his "social system," and in France those of Fourier and Saint Simon. The word remained constantly in use thereafter until Marx denounced all socialism before his days as unscientific socialism. "Scientific socialism" of Karl Marx bases itself on interpreting all previous history as a struggle of the oppressed classes to free themselves from the tyranny of the oppressors. The oppressors, however,

---

1. *Encyclopaedia Britannica*, 14th edition, article "Socialism".

have always found new weapons for exploitation. Their latest achievement is the capitalist organisation in which entrepreneurs possessing all means of production force the labourers to accept wages which just help them keep the soul and body together. For the exploitation, this is the beginning of the end. Soon a "conscious minority" of labourers recognises the role that "history" wants them to play. They persuade and force their class to take control of all the means of production. Thus begins the "dictatorship of the proletariat". It is prophesied that this would be a passing phase in the supreme consummation of communism. When the oppressor class is liquidated, a classless society would come into being. The members will give to the society all that they can in the shape of services, and will receive from it all that they need. In the end when communism begins working smoothly, there would be no need of a State, and it would "wither away" by itself.

The difference between socialism and communism is one of method and degree of achievement. Socialism seeks to achieve collective control without resort to revolution. Socialism is a considerable parliamentary force in various countries. Its devotees hope to gain power and collectivise productive instruments in an evolutionary process. The communists denounce them with an invective as unmeasured as used against the capitalists. The communists consider revolution essential for attaining communism. The second difference is that the individuals, instead of receiving from the society all that 'they need," would receive under socialism according to their output of work. Russia is communist in the sense that she achieved socialisation by revolutionary means; but is socialist in the sense that she has found payment to individuals according to what they "need" impracticable, and pays only according to what an individual "does". A further contention is that this too is a temporary phase and ultimately when socialism is firmly established and matured they will attain the communist principle of paying according to what men need. The prophet of this "scientific socialism" was Karl Marx whose theories need to be examined for a proper evaluation of socialism.

Marx, the Philosopher

Marx borrowed his dialectics from Hegel. Hegel took the word from the Greeks, for whom it was a process of arriving at truth by debate. He re-emphasised the value of fruitful contradiction. Save the idea, everything within itself contains not only itself but also its opposite. The conception of being contains within itself the conception of non-being, and from the conflict of opposites contained within a thing emerges the possibility of becoming. Thus every thesis contains within itself an antithesis and the conflict between the two produces a synthesis higher than the first thesis. This synthesis, in its turn, is found to contain within itself its opposite leading to a higher synthesis. The conflict of opposites thus continually leads to progress.

Hegel's dialectic was one of thought. Marx made it a dialectic of matter. Idea for Marx was not the vital force it was for Hegel. According to Marx, ideas are no more than the abstract representation of the material word. All legal and political institutions as well as religious are the abstract projection of concrete material surroundings. Thus it is not the ideas that mould the world, but the material facts that create those ideas.

According to Marx's dialectic, material situations of each epoch produce class-antagonisms. There were freemen and slaves in ancient days, feudal lords and serfs in medieval age, and there are capitalists and labourers in modern times. The possessing classes have constantly endeavoured to retain their hold and exploit the have-nots. The exploited have sought to free themselves from this exploitation. All history is a history of this class-struggle, which assumes new forms with the changing circumstances of each epoch. This class-struggle is constantly evolving towards a higher synthesis when the instruments of production will not be owned by individuals but by the State, and the antagonism of classes will cease to exist. Capitalism brings nearer that consummation. Capitalism, on the one hand, accentuates the antagonism between the classes, and, on the other, its development leads to concentration of productive instruments in fewer and fewer hands till it becomes possible for the exploited masses to snatch the productive instruments and establish communism. This evolutionary interpretation of history leads to historical determinism. There is an inevitability in this process and capitalism must yield place to communism.

In this dialectical determinism—class-antagonisms leading to communism—capitalism becomes an historic necessity. It is an essential preliminary stage. If it is so, the Marxists should have welcomed capitalism like the gilded East which promises the day. But they denounce capitalism. In fact, in the word arimoury of communism there are few weapons as biting as tyranny, oppression and exploitation. They are all reserved for capitalism. There is a contradiction here between Marx the neo-Hegelian and Marx the communist prophet. With unmeasured invective, he denounces the same capitalism which his own theory shows not only inevitable but also benevolent, for it opens up the way for communism.

For dialectical materialism, class-struggle is the motive force behind all material progress. In "all hitherto existing societies" class-struggle has opened the way for the material evolution of man. This class-struggle continues until, with the "dictatorship of the proletariat," ushers in the classless society. This means, and the communists have never faced this point, that the motive force behind further material progress will disappear. The concept of history that Marx gives us is evolutionary only up to a point; beyond that the world becomes static and all material progress by the logic of the theory stops.

To Marxism the struggle of the classes is the dynamic of history. The oppressed class struggles against the domination of the master class and out of the conflict comes progress, one class replacing another as master in the rhythm, the dialectic of events. So natural a process is this discerned to be that Lenin, (in *Materialism and Empiro-Criticism*) equates the class- struggle with such physical and chemical forces as negative and positive electricity, and the combination and dissociation of atoms. Yet Marxism adduces the *end of the class war* through the triumph of the proletariat, which having no class beneath it to exploit ushers in the classless society. What then happens to history when the mainspring of its motion is removed?[2]

---

2. Lealie Paul. *Annihilation of Man, p. 85.*

Besides this, dialectical determinism shares the drawback of all determinist philosophy in that it leaves the individual at the mercy of a determining power. If scientifically determinism could be established, individuals will have to reconcile to it. But fortunately, for all men, Bergson gave an argument irrefutable rejecting biological determinism of Darwin. Darwin showed that man has evolved into what he is by a process of natural selection. All organic life, which is weak, would fail to adapt itself successfully with its surroundings and would die in the struggle for existence. So far as biological evolution is concerned there is no need to fight against it. But to proceed from this premises and declare that man is a mere determinate of the biological process is incompatible with man's capacity to remember things. Man's memory helps him in selecting his line of action whenever he has to choose from a number of alternatives. Bergson asked biological determinists to explain the existence of memory in man. That question still remains to be answered by them.

Dialectical determinism is even worse than the biological one. Individual was a unit in the struggle for existence. He is a fraction of a unit which carries on the class-struggle. His ideas, his achievements, his emotions, his preferences are all unimportant. They are a mere shadow of the material word. They play no part in shaping the world—except in so far as they contribute to the class-struggle and help the proletariat to establish their dictatorship. A philosophy that considers man and his idea—the essential greatness of man—to be of no consequence could not but lead to a social organisation in which liberty to think and speak, act and associate, is circumscribed within the close bounds of the communist philosophy.

Marx, the Historian

Philosophy of Marx, as we have seen, proceeds out of his interpretation of history. Let us see if history bears out Marx in his interpretation. This is what Marx writes:

> The history of all hitherto existing societies is the history of class-struggles.
>
> Freeman and slave, patrician, and plebeian, lord and serf, guildmaster and journeyman, in a word, oppressor and the oppressed,

stood in the constant opposition to one another, carried on an uninterrupted, now hidden; now open, fight—a fight that each time ended either in a revolutionary reconstitution of society at large or in the common ruin of the contending classes.

In the earlier epochs of history, we find almost everywhere a complicated arrangement of society into various orders, a manifold gradation of social rank. In ancient Rome we have patricians, knights, plebeians, slaves: in the Middle Ages, feudal lords, vassals, guildmasters, journeymen, apprentices, serfs; in almost all these classes, again, subordinate gradation.

The modern bourgeois society that has pouted from the ruins of feudal society has not done away with class antagonisms. It has but established new classes, new conditions of oppression, new forms of struggle in place of the old ones.

Our epoch, the epoch of the bourgeoisie, possesses, however, this distinctive feature: it has simplified the class antagonisms. Society as a whole is more and more splitting into two great hostile camps, into two great classes, directly facing each other, bourgeoisie and proletariat.[3]

It is very revealing to see how Marx came by this interpretation of history. In 1831 in Lyons there took place a workers' uprising, closely followed by another in England which culminated in the chartist agitation. "These new facts," writes Engels, "compelled a re-examination of the whole of history, and then it appeared that *all* [italics Engels's] excepting only very ancient society, was the history of class-struggles."[4]

It means that Marx, impressed by the two risings in Lyons and England, wanted to see them as a continuation of an historical process. No wonder, he found that all history was made up of class-struggles, beginning from the days when there were freemen and slaves. "All perception," writes Williams, "is apperception."

That there were gradations in society all through the various epochs nobody can deny, as there are still even in Russia as we will soon see. But that there was an "uninterrupted" fight between the various classes, and that this fight constitutes the whole of history, is not borne out by history itself. Let us take freemen and slaves, because this is the oldest gradation of society which persists even today in certain countries. Does the history of any one country show that the slaves, as a class, ever struggled to

3 *Manifesto of the Communist Party*, opening paragraphs.

4. *Entwicklung*, p. 31.

wrest their independence? Nowhere does history provide any evidence that the slaves anywhere at any time considered themselves a class in the Marxist sense.

The ultimate liberation of slaves in most countries was not the result of the slaves struggle for it. It was the result of the efforts of noble-spirited men, like Browne and Lincoln, that they became free. Reading the history of the liberation of slaves, one is impressed by the total absence of the class-struggle. Men like William Browne, who was a free trader, and, therefore, an exploiter, fight for their liberty and give away their lives in the noble cause. What place in the class-struggle would the communists assign to Browne? When he waited in Harper's Ferry through the last three restless days of his struggle waiting for the slaves to rise, why did they fail to do so? If the slaves had been class-conscious, they would never have missed the opportunity.

When Alexander invaded Persia both Darius and Alexander had their slaves, but it was not a war between slaves and freemen or any other "classes". The slaves of Alexander fought for him hoping to gain material benefit from his conquest, and the slaves of Darius defended Persia hoping to retain the benefits they received from their master. The virility of Alexander's soldiers and better striking power of his war weapons gave victory to him. He passed on to India marching on the routes which were to be treaded by a score of subsequent invaders. Yet the war between Alexander and Porus was not a war between the "exploiters" and the "exploited". Both of them in the one camp fought with both of them in the other. It was a war to win wealth and glory on the one hand and retain independence on the other. Similarly, neither the Roman conquest of North Africa nor of England can be explained in terms of class-struggle. Patricians as well as plebeians won fortune by the Roman conquest, and lost by its liquidation. Muhammad was born in a family who were custodians of the Ka bah. In terms of material gains, he could have got anything for relinquishing the preaching of his religion. He was offered wealth and women if he desisted, and warm, unrelenting opposition if he persisted. "If you place the sun on my one hand," replied Muḥammad, " and the moon on the other, I shall not desist from preaching what God asks me to preach." According to the Marxists, ideas do not affect world history. But here was an idea of a man expressed in these words, which shaped his conduct and made history for a thousand years. Muḥammad's slaves fought for Muḥammad against all those people who had decided to exterminate Islam. Muhammad still has slaves: four hundred millions of them. The greatest honour for each one of them is that he is Muhammad's slave. Pick up any one of them and place the sun on his one hand and the moon on his other and ask him to go against his Master. He would not do it. Which class-struggle would explain this phenomenon?

Or what class-struggle would explain the downfall of Islam? Their internecine wars in Spain leading to their extermination and expulsion. To which "oppressed" class did Hulagu belong? Why did he destroy the Abbasids? Why was the voice of Musalmans so feeble for the last several centuries? Why is life coming back to them?

Or what led to the defeat of the Spanish Armada which decided that England shall build a world empire? Why don't the labourers of Britain join hands with the labourers in colonies and liquidate this empire? "Workers of the world, unite," cired Marx. But they don't. Workers of Germany fought against the workers of England, America and Russia. Labourers of England do not join with the labourers of the Empire to liquidate her. They know they have not "only their chains to loose". The English labourers fear the loss of bread and butter with the liquidation of the British Empire.

There are untouchables in India. An equally oppressed class of millions would be difficult to find in the world. Yet, not to speak of world history, they have not made a single page in the Indian history. Professor Brij Narain has tried to see if class-struggle applies to Indian history.[5] He has come to the conclusion: "If all history is class-struggle, India has no history at all." Why has this ancient land of culture been deprived of the benefit of history?

5. Cf. Brij Narain, *Indian Socialism*, Chap 3: also *idem*, *Marxism is Dead*, Chap. 4

What class-struggle led to the two world wars? Why Turkey joined Germany in the First World War and sided the Allies in the Second? Why did the arch-capitalist U.S.A. join hands with the Socialist Russia to fight against Germany in the Second World War? This alignment of powers is the very negation of class-struggle if ever there was any.

Modern society has been largely shaped by the inductive method of acquiring knowledge. The ascendancy of Europe in industry and commerce, arts and sciences, proceeds out of this one idea brought to Europe by Roger Bacon from the Arab universities of Spain. How can the insistence of Roger Bacon on the inductive method (or similar insistence by his later namesake Lord Bacon) be explained in terms of class-struggle?

Material considerations have always been one of the principal motives of common man.? They have made the individual exert for his personal gains irrespective of the class to which he belongs. It has not been a class-struggle but a struggle for existence: a struggle of "each against all". Very rarely has there been in history a conscious struggle of one class against another. In the struggle for existence, patricians and plebeians, lords and serfs, guildmasters and journey-men have struggled much more against each other than against their opposite classes.

That there have always been gradations in society, is correct. That material motives have shaped much of history, is equally so. But that "history of all hitherto existing societies is the history of class-struggle," is just not borne out by history itself.

Marx, the Economist

Just as Marx derived his dialectic from Hegel he borrowed his theory of value from Ricardo.

The labour theory of value can be traced back to Adam Smith. "The value of any commodity," he wrote,"....to the person who possesses it, and who means not to use or consume it himself, but to exchange it for other commodities is equal to the quantity of labour which it enables him to purchase or command.

Labour, therefore, is the real measure of the exchangeable value of all commodities."[6]

Ricardo inherited his theory from Adam Smith. He asserted that labour alone creates value and conceded that the value of a small number of commodities is also determined by scarcity.

The difference between Marx and Ricardo is that Marx recognises *manual* labour as the sole creator of value. The labour of middlemen and merchants, of entrepreneurs, and organisers, is not recognised as an addition to the value of goods. "As values, commodities are only definite masses of congealed labour-time."[7]

Marx distinguishes between the use value and the exchange value. Air, for instance, has great use value, but it seldom has exchange value. On the other hand, nothing has exchange value if it has no use value. What is a thing's exchange value? "If we leave out of account the use value of commodities," writes Marx, "they have only one common property left, that of being products of labour."[8]

Marx admists that labour differs in quality. It is easy enough to measure the quantity of labour according to the number of hours put in, but how to measure the quality of labour in the absence of exchange? He meets this difficulty by postulating a hypothetical unit or labour value based on socially necessary labour. "The labour-time socially necessary is that required to produce an article under the normal conditions of production, and with an average degree of skill and intensity prevalent at the time."[9]

This hypothetical unit of labour value is measured in the present system by way of wages which ultimately depend upon the prices which the products of labour would fetch in the market. But Marx denounces both market and wages as instruments of exploitation. In the absence of these instruments, we are left without any means of measuring the "socially necessary labour". How to measure the difference between skilled and unskilled

---

6. Adam Smith. *The Wealth of Nations*, Book I, Chap.5.
7. Karl Marx. *Das Kapital*, Alfred Knoll edition. Vol. I, p.6.
8. Ibid., p.4.
9. Ibid., p.6.

labour? "Skilled labour," writes Marx, "counts only as ordinary labour intensified, or as multiplied simple labour, a given quantity of skilled labour being equal to a great quantity of simple labour. Experience shows that this reduction is constantly made."[10]

Marx is right in asserting that this reduction is always made. But this reduction is made under conditions of demand and supply, where exchange is permitted, and money plays the role of the measure of value. In the absence of all these, how are we to find a measure of value, is what Marx fails to answer. "It is essential," as Mr. Joseph points out, "for Marx's arguments to show that reduction can be made without considering the price of the commodities, but he cannot show it."[11] It is essential for a prophet of social justice to meet the economic difficulties that confront his teachings. But Marx is not concerned with the economic implications even though they may make his theory unpractical. "He is not concerned," Mr. Lindsay points out, "to give a formula which will enable us to predict what a commodity will fetch, but to tell us under what conditions it will fetch will be what it is worth."[12]

The fact is that Karl Marx did not understand the important economic role played by the entrepreneur and those engaged in exchange. He did not realise that coal being dug in the coal pit, cloth manufactured in the factory and wheat produced in the farm would be useless if they were not transported and brought to those who need to warm their hearths, wear shirts and eat bread. Whoever brings the producers and the consumers together performs as valuable a service as the man who produces the thing. Marx was convinced not as an economist but as a social prophet that merchants eat up what should have gone to the labourers. "The merchant" explains Marx, "may be regarded as a machine which reduces a useless expenditure of energy which helps to set free some time for production."[13] But if he sets free some time for production, his is not a useless expenditure of energy. A merchant

10. Ibid., p.11.
11. H. W. B. Joseph, *The Labour Theory of Value in Karl Marx* p. 42.
12. A. D. Lindsay, *Karl Mark's Capital*, p. 75.
13. Karl Marx, op. cit., Vol II, p. 142.

does more. He carries production to consumers without which all production would be a wastage of labour.

Karl Marx saw around him exploitation. He did not try to analyse at what point exploitation comes in. He saw that labour did produce value, but he saw that labour was the most ill used class of men. He concluded that manual labour alone produces value.

Nobody can deny that there is exploitation in capitalism. But it does not enter through the services of the entrepreneur, nor that of the merchant or the middleman. They all perform services as valuable, at least, as the labourer himself. Exploitation enters capitalism via the institution of banks and the rate of interest, as we have already seen. If Labour Theory of Value were slightly amended, it could gain universal recognition. Include in labour all kinds of it whether it be that of the labourer proper, or the middleman, or the merchant, or the entrepreneur, or even the capitalist who forwards capital and undertakes to run the risk and get reward according to the gains of business for he would have to undertake the labour of supervision to see that his capital is properly used. Use labour in this wide sense and then, of course labour alone is the source of value. But in its present shape the theory is not tenable.

Marx, The Prophet

A fundamental prophecy of Marx was the shape that capitalism would assume in its evolutionary process, based on his interpretation of history. He predicted that capital would in future be concentrated in fewer and fewer hands and would thus make it easy for the proletariat to snatch control of productive instruments. If this prophecy could be shown to have been fulfilled, the whole of his conception of class-struggle and dialectical materialism would be vindicated. It is indeed an acid test.

The facts of the situation reveal that capitalism has developed on lines which Marx altogether failed to foresee. Capital for a little time, no doubt, continued to concentrate in fewer and fewer hands, but soon the lesser capitalists who had been knocked out, instead of joining the proletariat, invented the Joint Stock Company. They invested their own small resourcess, and asked the general public to purchase shares of very small denominations which they could with their slender savings. Even the labourers saved a little from their wages and purchased shares and bonds. The result was that, instead of the bourgeoisie strengthening the ranks of the proletariat, the proletariat have joined the bourgeoisie. "It is estimated that the number of small stock-holders in the United States is over 10,000,000 [1928]. Large numbers of workers have holdings in the concerns which employ them. In some cases thousands of workers contribute to nourish capitalistic enterprises and the members of the corporations they serve. In one large motor concern, over 90% of the employees are buying stock on the instalment plan. In another, company's employees doubled in one year their holdings of its stock. The capitalist system is indeed built pyramidwise, but instead of coming to a last hopeless attempt to stand upon its apex, according to the Marxist vision, it broadens its basis more than it raises its altitude. The original socialist predictions have been falsified, with the usual irony of human anticipation."[14]

This is not merely one prophecy gone wrong, but is, by implication, a factual refutation of the entire conception that led to it, viz. dialectical materialism.

There is an interesting prophecy of Marx that if slavery be abolished North America would be wiped off the map of nations. "Without slavery," wrote Marx, "you have no cotton, without cotton you have no modern industry. It is slavery that has given the colonies their value; it is the colonies that have created world trade; and it is the world trade that is the pre-condition of large-scale industry. Thus slavery is an economic category of the greatest importance. Without slavery, North America, the most progressive of countries, would be transformed into a patriarchal country. Wipe out North America from the map of the world, and you will have anarchy—the complete decay of modern commerce and civilisation. Abolish slavery and you will have wiped America off the map of nations."[15]

14. *Encyclopaedia Britannica*. 14the edition, article "Capitalism".
15. Karl Marx, *The Poverty of Philosophy*, p. 121.

America has abolished slavery and yet America, instead of being "wiped off the map of nations," is the greatest nation today in the world. The quotation incidentally shows the characteristic manner of Marx's arguments. His was a single-track mind. He saw one factor and made a prophecy, but missed too many others and the prophecy would turn out wrong.

Marx prophesied the growing misery of the workers. "Along with the constantly diminishing number of the magnates of capital" he wrote, "who usurp and monopolize all advantages of this process of transformation, grows the mass of misery, oppression, slavery, degradation, exploitation,"[16] But, due to the influence of trade unions on the one side and social legislation on the other, the standard of living of workers has enormously improved since Marx wrote. If Marx had been alive today, he would have been surprised to see labourers possessing their own automobiles. Communists try to save Marx by arguing that his predictions would have been correct if capitalism had not been improved. But that amounts to saying that Marx would have been correct if he had foreseen facts which he did not foresee!

According to the Marxist analysis, England should have been the first country to go red. England started the Industrial Revolution and, until after the First World War, she was the leading industrial country in the world. An American journalist questioned Marx about communism in 1871: "Do you expect to see it in England?" Marx replied, "Sooner than in any other country."[17] Yet Russia has gone communist, England has not. And why has Russia gone *red?* According to dialectical materialism, communism comes after capitalism has run its full course. But Russia was the least capitalist country in Europe when she became a "socialist republic".

The Problem of Efficiency

The greatest problem in working out the communist system is the problem of efficiency. If you undertake to compensate all the needs of men you employ, irrespective of their output of work,

16. *Idem, Das Kapital,* Vol. I, Chap. 34.
17. Quoted by Father D'Arey. S.J. *in Christian Morals,* p. 172.

it becomes doubtful if the productive machine would at all be worked. Men work because of the incentive that their payment would be in accordance with their output. Equal wages, or more or less equal wages, to all would discount efficiency and be a premium on slipshod work. Efficient men would cease to be so because they are not rewarded for their efficiency; and inefficient men would not improve themselves because they are well paid for their bad work. That is why all economists predicted that communism is incapable of being worked efficiently.

Russia claims that she has put communism to practise and has achieved efficiency. It cannot be denied that Russia is an efficient productive machine. But her claim that she has translated Marxist theories into practice is not valid. She has attained efficiency by *discarding* Marxist canons of payment and substituting in its place the capitalist method of payment according to the output of each worker. Marx claimed that altruistic motives would provide incentive for efficiency; but Russia has found by trial and error that egoistic motives are the only practical incentive to efficiency.

Marxist principles envisage a moneyless economy. Where there is a "free utilisation of the resources of society," money, exchange and markets have no place. Indeed, Russia tried to work something on these lines. "It is estimated that in the spring of 1920 payments in kind by the State met at least half of the needs of the workers, and M. Larin, a high Soviet official, spoke with enthusiasm of the distribution of products of social labour among workers in accordance with their needs."[18] It was hoped at that time that even this small use of money would soon be unnecessary. "But one thing" explained Bucharin, "is clear: the better the workers are able to control production, the smaller would become the need for money, and in the end money would die out completely."[19]

In 1920 and first half of 1921, several decrees were issued in Russia to abolish money-economy. But the thing did not work and the trouble had to be reinstated. Money did not "die out

18. Brij Narain, *Marxism is Dead*, p. 108.
19. W.D. Cohn, *Kann das Geld Abgeschaft Werden*, P. 58.

completely" but came back completely. The function of the rouble was explained by V.I. Mezhlauk, chairman of the State Planning Commission:

> With the abolition of the card system, the rapid elimination of payments in kind and the abolition of two sets and even three sets of prices as the monetary system developed, the rouble is becoming the sole and effective means for the realisation of the socialist principle of payment for labour.[20]

So the rouble reappeared as the principle of payment for labour. With it returned efficiency and enabled Russia to build up a powerful fighting machine to throw back the German hordes from the Russian soil. Russia is efficient because she has introduced the capitalist method of payment according to the output of work—piece-wages and Stakhnovite movement. She will continue to go on producing more and more efficiently as long as she does not make the mistake of giving communism a trial once again.

Is Marxism Dead?

We have seen that one of the Marxist principles, viz. moneyless economy, has not been realised in practice, and the future holds out no promise that in this work-a-day world we shall ever establish a society which needs no money.

Closely linked with this, there was another Marxist principle: to take from everyone what he can give, and to pay to everyone what he needs. Let us see whether this has been realised in Russia, where it is sought to work out communist principles. We have already seen that the problem of efficiency forced Russia to employ egoistic rather than altruistic incentives for production. The result is that a great difference in the relative incomes of the people obtains. A French communist, Comrade Yvon, gives the following figures regarding the difference in income.[21]

---

20. Lawrence and Wishart. *Soviet Union*. pp. 378-88.
21. *Ce du'est devenue la Revolution Russ*, pp. 25-6.

		Highest and lowest	*Usual monthly*
Workers	....	from 80 to 400 R.	125 to 225 R.
Small employees	....	from 80 to 300 R.	130 to 225 R.
Maid-servants	....	from 50 to R plus board and lodging	
Employees and average technicians	....	from 300 to 800 R.	
Responsible administrators and specialists, high officials, some professors, artists, and writers		from 1500 to 10,000 R, and more; for some the monthly income is quoted at 20,000 to 30,000R.	
Workers's Pensions		from 25 to 80 R. per month without any privileges	
Pensions to widows of high officials and specialists		from 250 to 1000 R per month plus villas or apartments for life and scholarships for their children and sometimes even for their grand-children.	

According to Comrade Yvon's figures, the difference in income is as high as from 25 to 30,000 roubles (roughly from Rs. 5 to Rs. 6000). We are indeed very far away from Lenin's thesis of 1917: "The salaries of the highest officials should not exceed the average salary of a good worker."[22] It must be confessed that the difference very high in itself, is still less than the difference in capitalist countries where some people have incomes very much more than Rs. 6000 per month, and unemployment and uninsured workers may get nothing. It must also be confessed that although the lowest income of Rs. 5 is hoplessly small, it is likely to go on increasing with increases in Russia's productive capacity. But if it so happens as is likely, the upper limit will also almost correspondingly increase. There is no possibility that the enormous difference between the relative incomes might shrink. The need of efficiency would always force Russia, as it has hitherto done, to retain this difference. All claims that Russia ultimately would come back to communist payment have no validity. The trend in Russia is definitely to march away from communist payment.

If we leave aside the labourers' low pensions and high pays of officials and confine ourselves to the different incomes within a factory or a mine, they do not compare favourably with capitalist countries. In *The New International* for February 1936, Marx Eastman quotes an article by Leon Sedov:

In mines, a non-Stakhnovist miner gets from 400 to 500 roubles a month, a Stakhnovist more than 1,600 roubles. The auxiliary worker, who drives a team below, gets only 170 roubles if he is not a

22. *Pravda*, 20 April 1917.

Stakhnovist and 400 roubles if he is (*Pravda*, 16th November, 1935)—that is one worker gets about ten times as much as another. And 170 roubles by no means represent the lowest wages, but the *average* wage, according to the data of Soviet statistics. There are workers who earn no more than 150, 120 or even 100 roubles a month.... The examples we give by no means indicate the extreme limits in the two directions.... And if one takes the wages of specialists, the picture of the inequality becomes positively sinister. Ostrogliodov, the head engineer of a pit, who more than realizes the plan, gets 8,600 roubles a month, and he is a modest specialist whose wages cannot, therefore, be considered exceptional. Thus, engineers often earn from 80 to 100 times as much as an unskilled worker.

Marx Eastman cites a table of the relative difference in earnings of some "of our wealthier American companies" in *The New Republic* for 15 July 1936. From the table it appears that the ratio of the best paid officials to the worst-paid workers is 41 to 1 in the Chile Copper Co.; 51 to 1 in the Curtis Publishing Co.; 82 to 1 in Consolidated Oil. But head engineer Ostrogliadov gets eighty-six times as much pay as the lowest labourer in the pit.

Testimony of Webbs, whom no one can accuse of anything except over-partiality for Russia, runs: The maximum divergence of individual incomes in the U.S.S.R., taking the extreme instances, is probably as great as the corresponding divergence in incomes paid for actual participation in work, in Great Britain if not in the United States. It is not clear whether the divergence between the extreme instances in the Soviet Union is actually widening."[23]

Thus Russia, the only country which professes to work for Marxist ideal of payment, is as far away from it as England. And Webbs allow for the possibility that the divergence may even increase. However that may be, this is certain: one important Marxist principle has died out in Russia without there being any possibility of its revival—in spite of claims to the contrary.

Closely linked with it is the Marxist ideal of a classless society. Classless societies depend on more or less equal payments. When the divergence in income is as great as we have seen, to talk of classless society is to talk of Utopia. Professor Brij Narain in his scholarly work *Marxism is Dead* shows on the

23. Sydney and Beatrice Webbs, *Soviet Communism: A New Civilization*, p. 1207.

basis of irrefutable evidence that the real wages of the average factory worker in Russia are even less than the corresponding wages in Bombay and Lahore. Money wages, no doubt, are very much more; but real wages—determined by the price index are even worse. Imagine, on the one side, the living of an average labourer of Russia, easily imaginable since we know the living of an average factory labourer in Lahore, and read, on the other, this account of the comfortable life of Gay Payoo officials given by Andrew Smith and one is forced to believe that Russia is as much a classless society as England or Pakistan. This is how Smith describes the living of a G.P.U. official:

One day a friend of mine, who worked in a Gay Payoo factory, asked me to visit him in his apartment house restricted to Gay Payoo officials. The Gay Payoo has its own plants worked exclusively by prison labour under the supervision of experts, technicians and guards. In the course of a number of visits, I was invited into the home of one of the leading Gay Payoo officials living in the same house. He wanted to talk to me about the United States.

I was led into a gorgeous seven-room apartment equipped with its own kitchen and individual bathroom, with elevator service, telephones, steam heat, hot and cold water. My host lived there with his wife and two maid-servants. The couple had no children. The apartment consisted of a saloon or sitting-room, a dining-room, two master bedrooms and one bedroom for the two servants, an office or work-room for the master of the house, a room for card-playing and dancing and a summer porch. The apartment was sumptuously furnished with thickly upholstered chairs, soft couches and expensive antiques. Scattered throughout the suite were small hand-carved tables covered with beautifully coloured mosaics made of rare Ural stone. The parquet floors and the walls were covered with thick hand-woven oriental rugs. In odd corners one could see rich knick-knacks consisting of jewel boxes made of seashells, vases, hand-carved ash trays and oriental bric-a-brac. From the ceiling in each room hung a heavy crystal chandeliar. These were supplemented by more modern floor lamps, with cut glass and silk shades. The couple possessed a radio of Russian manufacturer and a German phonograph. On the floors of the master bedrooms were thick white bear skins. Rich Russian hand-made draperies hung about the walls to complete the picture. It was the most luxurious apartment I had ever seen, richer ever than the apartment of the wealthy business man in Pittsburgh for whom my wife had worked as a cook.

I found the lady of the house reclining in a soft easy chair in the sitting-room, reading a magazine. She held a gold-tipped cigarette in her soft white fingers. I could see her highly roughed finger nails. She had not spared either in making herself ready for that occasion and her eyebrows were carefully plucked in the most up-to-date manner. Her bleached hair was permanently waved *a la mode*.

Clad in a heavy, dark silk dress, cut very low, she wore silk stocking and high-heeled shoes to match. Occasionally, she glaced at her imported gold wrist watch and toyed with her pearl necklace. Heavy gold earrings hung almost to her shoulders. Her fingers were heavily ringed. Altogether, by her appearance and manners, she looked to me like a prostitute.

We were served in the brilliantly lighted dining-room, with delicacies which I have not seen in the Soviet Union. There was real tea served in delicate oriental cups, and poured from an enormous steaming silver samovar. The knives, forks and spoons were relics of the treasures of the defunct Russian aristocracy. There was a special silver service for each course. We had white bread, caviare, cheese, fresh radishes, salami, fish, fresh fruit, apples, pears, raspberry compote, delicious Russian candies and pastry, and cognac of the most ancient vintage.

In the course of the repast, my hostess consumed a most generous portion of the cognac. She began to talk hysterically and talk in loud tones. As we left the house after our visit I remarked sarcastically to my friend:

"And this is what the Russian workers have to slave for. And they call this a workers' country."

"This is nothing," my friend replied, "you ought to see what goes on when they throw one of their Gay Payoo parties."[24]

Of course this is not the highest limit. Above the G.P.U. officials are the higher officers with better emoluments. Lower down there are all grades of workers until we reach the lowest paid labourer with about 100 roubles. Lower down still are workers' pensions beginning from the lowest limit of 25 roubles. The result is that there are as many classes in Russia as there are anywhere else. There are first, second, and third classes in railways and cinemas and theatres and on the steamers just as they are in any capitalist country. And there are corresponding ranks in society which use the various grades of service. Mr. Sloan tries to explain it:

Certain readers may be surprised at my reference to first, second and third class on the steamers. When I add that in the trains services of the U.S.S.R. the same terms are also sometimes used certain of you may exclaim, "Oh, but I thought classes had been abolished in the U.S.S.R." Let me, therefore, at this point explain that when it is said that classes have been abolished in the U.S.S.R. this means that the

24. Andrew Smith, *I Was a Soviet Worker*, p. 45.

division of society into landlords, employers and working people has been abolished.[25]

Names do not matter. There are new divisions of society: party-bosses, high officials, managers, engineers, Stakhnovists, unskilled labourers. They all have different incomes and ranks. So even this Marxist principle, viz. classless society, has not been realised in Russia.

Three basic Marxist principles, viz. moneyless economy, payment according to need, and classless society, could not be translated into practice in spite of great efforts. Shall we conclude that Marxism is dead? We cannot. Not because the Russians still hope that at some future date they will be realised, for, we may be sure, that the problem of efficiency would never permit the Russians to work them out: but for a different reason. Marxism is not dead, because the Russians have put at least one Marxist principle into practice: They have nationalised almost all means of production and exchange. Instead of individuals owning land or industry the State owns (almost) everything and individuals work thereon and are paid according to their output. Instead of anybody working of another man everyone works for himself and the State. Communists generally argue that because of nationalisation there is no exploitation in Russia. "Exploitation" in Marxist terminology is closely linked with Labour Theory of Value. All value is produced by labour and anyone who gets advantage from another's labour exploits him. If we keep this definition in mind, it is difficult to prove absence of exploitation in Russia. It is true that no one can employ another, but there is a subtler way in which exploitation still continues. From where does, for instance, the G.P.U. official, whose luxurious apartment has been described above, gets his income? Does he labour? He obviously gets a huge salary from the State without *producing* anything. This means he takes away something which should have gone to the labourers who are the only producers in the Marxist sense. That is, he exploits. There is, however, another and very much vaster class of exploiters both in the Marxist as well as the Islamic sense. We are told by Gunther in *Inside Europe* that Russian

25. Pat Sloan. *Russia Without Illusions*, p. 62.

banks in order to attract deposits pay a high interest. "There is no limit," he writes, "to the amount of capital any one may accumulate. There are no opportunities for investment, however, except in state bonds. The bonds pay interest, exactly as do bonds in capitalist countries and a good rate too— eight per cent. Savings banks are encouraged and in 1935 no fewer than forty-three million depositors throughout the Soviet Union used them. They pay eight to ten per cent interest."[26] It is obvious that all these millions of investors are exploiters getting interest which should have gone to the labourers who are the only creators of value. If in spite of that I suggest that Marxism is not dead, I mean that the instruments of production can be and have been socialised. This much of Marxism lives; all else both in theory and practice has died out. What is left for us to see is whether this residue of Marxism that lives is good—conductive to the happiness of the average man and woman. Before we can give our verdict, we should see both the assets and the liabilities of socialisation of the instruments of production.

Achievements of Socialism

Socialisation of instruments of production has enabled Soviet Russia to take long strides in the domain of production, industrial as well as agricultural, and has provided her with enough resources to make magnificent achievements in the fields of education, medical facilities and military might.

The leaders of Soviet Russia brought to bear almost superhuman planning and Herculean power of execution. Five-year plans were made, fixing targets for each industry and every plant, which were very often fulfilled.

The first five-year plan, on which work started in 1929 aimed to introduce large-scale collective farming in the domain of agriculture and to extend industrial production to such an extent that the U.S.S.R. may become in the main an industrial instead of an agrarian country. In four years 94% of the industrial target was fulfilled. The volume of industrial production had increased three times compared to that of 1913 and had doubled compared to that of 1928. The ratio of industrial production to total national

26. Gunther, *Inside Europe*, p. 511.

production rose from 48% at the beginning of the plan to 75% at the end of the fourth year. In the first five-year plan, 20,000 collective farms and 5,000 grain-growing and livestock-breeding farms were established. Collective farms now covered 70% of the peasant acreage.

The second five-year plan covered the period 1932-7. During this period the value of industrial production increased from 43,000 million to 96,000 million roubles. "Compared to 1913, the output of electricity increased 17.3 times by 1936 reaching 32,000 million kilowatt-hours."[27] With the increase in electric energy, most of the laborious industrial processes could be mechanised. A large quantity of agricultural machinery was also produced. "By 1938 Soviet agriculture had 483,000 tractors totalling 9,256,000 horse-power, 153,000 combines, 130,000 complex and semi-complex threshers, 193,000 trucks,"[28]

With this material advancement, efforts were made to raise the cultural level of the people. The number of school pupils increased from 23 million in 1933 to 40 million in 1938. University students numbered 550,000. In 1938, Soviet Russia had "70,000 public libraries, 95,000 club establishments, 790 theaters and 30,400 cinema installations, 8500 newspapers were published with a total circulation of 7000 millions"[29] During the first and second five year plans, 1,500,000 specialists were trained, of whom women were a considerable number. "In the state budget, expenditures for social and cultural measures increased from 5,839.9 million roubles in 1933 to 35,202.5 million roubles in 1938."[30] A similar improvement is claimed in the number of parks and sanitoria, hospitals and books.

The third five-year plan, which aimed at further strides in the industrial field, was cut short on account of the Second World War, during which a considerable quantity of Russia's agricultural and industrial equipment was destroyed. With the close of the war, new plans are well under way to make up the

27. A. Kursky. *Planned Economy in the U.S.S.R.*, p. 9.
28. Ibid.
29. Ibid., p. 11.
30. Ibid., p. 18.

losses sustained during the war; and to raise industrial production to hitherto unrelated targets in any capitalist country.

This is how Russian propaganda narrates the remarkable story of the industrial and cultural attainments of the Soviet Union. We have no means to verify the figures given. For the sake of our argument we will assume they are correct. But even if they are, we cannot vote for the Soviet system before we have seen the other side of the picture as well.

The Price of Socialism

The price of this achievement has been paid in terms of the suppression of personal liberty. Through the press, the radio and the school, which are completely controlled, the people are taught the single-track ideas of Marx as interpreted by the chief party boss. Nobody has the power to question or criticize these ideas on the pain of being liquidated as a "reactionary". The method of the socialists in dealing with those who differ from them is a continuation of Marx's unscientific temper. Ruhle, Marx's devoted biographer, quotes Carl Schurz, who was present at the Cologne Congress of 1849: "never have I seen anyone whose manner was more insufferably arrogant. He would not give a moment's consideration to any opinion that differed from his own. He treated with contempt everyone who contradicted him. Arguments that were not to his taste were answered either by mordent sarcasms upon the speaker's lamentable ignorance or else by casting suspicion on the motives of his adversary."[31] Marx did not command the power of shooting the man, otherwise, doubtless, he would have done it. But socialist Russia commands that power and has never failed in silencing opposition with a bit of lead.

It is difficult to gather complete figures of all those who have died in Russia because of their opinions. The estimate given by Iljin in *The World on the Brink of the Abyss*, which is now out of date, is that 1,860,000 people have been killed out of which there were 28 bishops, 1200 priests, 6,000 teachers and professors,

---

31. Otto Ruhle, *Karl Marx, His Life and Work* (translated by Eden and Paul), p. 157.

8800 doctors, 192,000 workmen and 815,000 peasants. This estimate is corroborated by W.H. Chamberlain, who represented *The Christian Science Monitor* in Russia from 1922 to 1934. According to him, the number of Soviet citizens who have been "deprived of liberty without anything that could plausibly be called 'due process of law' can be scarcely less than two million"[32]

The liquidation of kulaks has entailed the life of several hundred thousand peasants. Even the best admirers of Russia have found it difficult to defend the liquidation of kulaks. An American communist describes it as "the most spectacular act of ruthlessness which occurred in these years"[33]. Even the Webbs were compelled to confess, "The sum of human suffering involved is beyond all computation."[34]

It is not only the people who differ from the government policy that run the risk of their life. Anyone, even though he may have devoted his life for communism, risks his life in a country where the whim and convenience of a dictator take the place of normal courts of law. "The list of those shot," writes Marx Eastman, "Or who shot themselves or who were named as implicated with the victims, comprises—with a single exception—everyone of the eminent Bolsheviks who sat with Stalin around the council table of Lenin: Trotsky, Zinoviev, Kanemew, Rykov, Bukharin, Radek, Sokolnikov, Piatakov (mentioned in Lenin's testament as among the ablest), Yevdokimov, Smiroy (once known as 'the Lenon of Siberia'), Tomsky (Head of the Federation of Labour), Serebriakov (Stalin's predecessor as secretary of the party) and several others only a little less eminent."[35] "Ten Judases out of twelve is a rather high proportion for a new religion," remarks Arnold Lunn.[36]

It is violence and terror that has assumed the place of law in Russia. Not that there are no law-courts in Russia. But the law-courts function subject to the requirements of violence and terror.

---

32. W.H. Chamberlain, *Russia's Iron Age*, p. 157.
33. A.L. Strong quoted by Eugene Loyns, *Assignment in Utopia*, p. 283.
34. Sidney and Beatrice Webbs, op. cit., p. 567.
35. Marx Eastman, *Harper's Magazine*, Feb. 1937, p. 313.
36. Arnold Lunn, *Revolutionary Socialism*, p. 156.

We have testimony for it of no less a person than Lenin himself. In his famous letter published in *The Bolshevik* for 31 October 1920, he wrote: "The legal trial is not intended to replace terrorism; to make such a profession would be deception of others or oneself; but to base terrorism firmly on a fundamental principle and give it a legal form, unambiguous, without dishonesty or embellishment."

Latsis, statistician to the Russian government, writes:

> We are out to destroy the bourgeoisie as a class. Hence, whenever a bourgeois is under examination the first step should be not to endeavour to discover material of proof that the accused has opposed the Soviet government, whether verbally or actually, but to put to the witness the three questions: "To what class does the accused belong?" What is his origin?" and "describe his upbringing, education and profession." Solely in accordance with the answers to these three questions should his fate be decided. For this is what "Red Terror" means and what it implies.[37]

So the demands of law are reduced to this: put three questions to a witness—possibly a government agent—and if his answers are against the accused, he is shot. Of course, when the great Bolsheviks, like Zinoviev and Bukharin, were purged, this simple process was not adopted. But the alternative was even more inhuman. It is difficult to explain the process involved in the short span of a chapter. Readers interested in the confusing problem of purges would find the only convincing explanation hitherto given in *Man and Politics* by Luis Fischer.

The law in Russia—or its negation—sees to it that all opposition and difference of opinion are silenced for ever. The remaining citizens are coached in school, through press and radio that Soviet Russia is the noblest country in the world and the capitalist world is a hell. They naturally believe it, for they have no sources to verify that knowledge independently. This regimentation of ideas on the one hand and the absence of personal security and personal freedom on the other are the evils of Soviet Russia.

---

37. S. P. Heigounov, *The Red Terror in Russia*, p. 39.

The Unsocial Socialism

Against the material achievements of Russia must be placed the absence of personal liberty and security. Probably, the abolition on unemployment must be considered the greatest achievement of Russia. Any man who wants to work can find work in the Soviet State. Of course, if he is inefficient and unskilled, his wages would be just enough to provide him with the minimum necessities. With further development of Russian industries, the wages are likely to improve. Besides, the chances of acquiring skill and knowledge are also likely to be extended until they may even cover the entire population. But man does not live by bread alone. He also seeks liberty to think, speak and act as he pleases. This freedom cannot be given to individuals in a dictatorial State. No dictatorship can even function efficiently without a spy system and concentration camps where men may be sent without trial. Can anyone feel secure when G.P.U. hounds him through day and night? The democratic system provides one the guarantee that he would not be punished unless the guilt has been proved against him beyond any doubt and he is given every opportunity to defend himself. The law-court presumes him innocent until the guilt is established. He enjoys this presumption even against the State. The absence of personal security and liberty in the Soviet system makes it a highly unsocial system. Bread is not worth much when one is denied the protection of law.

> The experience of the Soviet Union and of all dictatorships has demonstrated that without freedom there can be no full stomachs. What is a job when you can be lifted out of it by the secret police on no charge or on an unknown charge and imprisoned and shot without open trial and without friends and relatives knowing anything about you? Sometimes a Soviet official disappears in the night. His wife immediately begins leaving food parcels for him at the G.P.U. prison. She has asked no questions because she will get no answers. Then, one day, the guard at the gate rejects her parcel. That is how she learns that her husband has been shot.[38]

The misery of man has not ended in Russia. That system alone can bring happiness to man which, besides providing him bread and butter, assures him of the freedom to think, to speak

38. Luis Fischer. *Men and Politics*, p. 316.

and act, to assemble and oppose even the government, and assures him the protection of his person. Socialism is not that system.

There is only one proposition left for us to examine. Is it possible simultaneously to nationalise all instruments of production and retain liberal democratic institutions? Fischer, one of the most sympathetic students of Russia, gives an emphatic No. When all economic power is centralised in the hands of the State, the individual must become small by contrast. That all-powerful State must needs exercise dictatorial power to work the huge productive machine efficiently. The centralisation of economic functions cannot but result in the centralisation of power, and the chief executive must become a dictator. Indeed, this is the one important lesson that Russia has to teach. In socialist economic system, State does not "wither away"; it becomes a Super State. Social problems of man cannot be solved by socialism.

> To jump from the monism of uncontrolled capitalism to the monism of uncontrolled state ownership, or state domination of all property, industry and finance is no solution. In fact it is highly dangerous. Even in countries where there is a stronger tradition of democracy and personal freedom than in Russia and Germany the omnipotent state—omnipotent because it owned and ran everything—might still become a menace to liberty. I fear the strong state. The individual is at its mercy. When a state is the employer of all no strikes are permitted. Where the state owns everything, how can private individuals own the press? If the Government owns the press, how can one criticize the State?[39]

To become unsocial is in the very nature of socialism!

39. Ibid., p.624.

Chapter 4

Zakāt

The Meaning of Zakāt. Importance of Zākat. Its Purpose. Its Special Contribution. Conventional Basis of Assessment. An Answer to Professor Smith. Zakāt for Today.

The Meaning of Zakāt

Zakāt literaly means purification. Technically, it is a tax on the wealthy to provide social justice. Zakāt effects purification in three directions. Its work covers the moral, the economic and the social spheres. In the moral sphere, it washes away greed and acquisitiveness of the wealthy, makes them alive to and responsible for solving the problem of poverty. It frees the spirit of man from the hold of wealth which grows tighter in direct proportion to the greed of man. The wealthy are made responsible individually and collectively through the State to see to it that the elementary necessities of life are provided to all the members of the nation. The stakes are made considerably greater than social security for the Musalmans. To the Musalman this life is an opportunity given him to qualify himself for a happier life beyond the grave. And the Qur'ān has warned him:

By no means shall ye
Attain righteousness unless
Ye give (freely) of that
Which ye love, and whatever

Ye give, of a truth
God knoweth it well.[1]

Until wealth, which is so dear to the wealthy, is given away freely, the cause of social security will not be advanced; but, what is more, they will not "attain righteousness".

Secondly, Zakāt purifies wealth itself of its evil tendency to gather more and more in fewer and fewer hands on account of unequal opportunities which men enjoy. Zakāt takes away from the few their surplus wealth and gives it to the many to provide necessities of life to them. Wealth is no longer the demon for which men work on, even when they no longer need it. Welfare is the end and not wealth. But unlike Ruskin,[2] who made that distinction in the nineteenth century, Islam does not believe that a pound earned is a pound taken away from someone else's pocket. According to Islam, the productive earning of wealth enriches the whole community. Earning of wealth is therefore encouraged:

And when the Prayer
Is finished, then disperse
Ye through the land
And seek of the Bounty
Of God: and celebrate
The praises of God
Often (and without stint)
That ye may prosper.[3]

So repeatedly does the Qur'ān order seeking "the Bounty of God" that the Prophet made it a duty for the Musalmans only next in importance to prayer: "The Prophet of God (peace and blessings of God be upon him), said, 'Earning of wealth by honest means is next in importance only to the duty of prayer.'"[4] When everyone has done his best to earn wealth, the Qur'ān comes forth to inform him:

And in their wealth
Is the right of him
Who asks, and him
Who is needy.[5]

---

1. iii. 92.
2. Ruskin. *Unto This Last.*
3. The Qur'ān, lxii 10.
4. *Kanz-ul-'Ummāl*, Vol. II.
5. li. 19.

The third domain in which the institution of Zakāt performs its purifying process is the entire social sphere. A nation of paupers on the one side and millionaires on the other is the most unfortunate of nations. Not only because the vast majority of the population is underfed, underclothed, unhealthy, uneducated and therefore inefficient, but also because, as a consequence, industry and trade of that nation stagnate and get blocked. The crises occur. When the vast majority of the nation has no purchasing power, who can purchase the goods which the factories are turning out and the good things of life which the shopkeepers display in their show-cases? What can the factories do except stopping production when there is no market for the accumulated stock? And this causes unemployment and therefore reduces puchasing power. The vicious circle continues until the dark clouds of poverty gather thick and cover the whole nation. Even the millionaires become the poorer for it. Not so in Islam. Islam does not object to the earning for millions; but makes it the duty of the State to see to it that not a single man is left unprovided with the elementary necessities of life in the whole country. The well-to-do are to pay for it. When food, clothing, shelter, education and medical aid are provided to the entire nation, their efficiency as well as their standard of living improves. Their efficiency brings them higher wages by which they try to live as well as they can afford. The result is an increase in the demand of things that the factories produce and the shopkeepers sell. The result is an extension of production; therefore more employment, therefore more purchasing power, therefore still more employment until the entire nation becomes prosperous. In spite of having paid the heavy duty of Zakāt, the wealthy donot become poor; they rather go on getting further wealth on account of the extension of trade and industry. That is why the Qur'ān has contrasted charity with interest:

God will deprive
Usury of all blessing,
But will give increase
For deeds of charity:
For He loveth not

Creatures ungrateful
And wicked.[6]

We have seen in our discussion on interest that "usury" works as a positive brake and retards the extension of production and actually deprives the economic system "of all blessing". We have seen above how *charity organised as a religious duty on a national basis consciously aiming at social justice*, and that, incidentally, would be a defintion of Zakāt, actually brings "increase" in the material welfare of the whole community—blessing "him who giveth and him who taketh".

Importance of Zakāt

The order to pay Zakāt runs like a refrain in the Qur'ān, where it is generally mentioned alongwith the order to establish prayer. There are at least twenty-seven passages[7] in the Qur'ān where the two orders occur jointly. This is besides scores of verses in which only charity is enjoined:

The parable of those
Who spend their substance
In the way of God is that
Of a grain of corn: it groweth
Seven ears, and each ear
Hath a hundred grains.
God giveth manifold increase
To whom He pleaseth:
For God careth for all
And knoweth all things.
Those who spend
Their substance in the cause
Of God, and follow not up
Their gifts with reminder
Of their generosity
Or with injury,—for them
Their reward is with their Lord:
On them shall be no fear
Nor shall they grieve.[8]

The verses that follow explain in the form of beautiful parables the material, moral and spiritual blessings that charity

6. ii. 276.
7. Cf. M. Muhammad Ali, *Islam and the World*, p. 463 in.
8. ii. 261 - 262.

brings in its wake (ii. 264-266). It is explicitly stated that charity should only be given from wealth earned by honourable means (ii. 267); and it is emphasised that the giving of charity does not make anyone poor:

> The Evil One threatens
> You with poverty
> And bids you to conduct
> Unseemly. God promiseth
> You with forgiveness
> And bounties.
> And God careth for all
> And He knoweth all things.[9]

These are the orders for optional individual charity as distinguished from obligatory collective charity or Zakāt and even the former is not so very optional because:

> By no means shall ye
> Attain righteousness unless
> Ye give (freely) of that
> Which ye love: and whatever
> Ye give, of a truth
> God knoweth it well.[10]

To this optional charity, although it is very important as a means of moral elevation and would therefore be necessary of any system aiming at the real welfare of man, we shall give no more space because it can only touch the fringe of the problem of mass poverty. Unlike other religions, Islam does not stay at charity. It enjoins upon the Musalmans nation-wide Zakāt to eradicate poverty. As already stated, at least twenty-seven times the order to pay Zakāt is repeated in the Qur'ān, and very significantly, along with the order to establish prayer. The spiritual discipline inculcated by prayer would lose its practical signficance if men did nothing to organise themselves to root out poverty and social injustice. The brotherhood of man is not realised only by bowing together of the ruler and the subject, the lord and the peasant, the factory-owner and the wage-earner shoulder to shoulder before One God, but is established on a firm foundation even outside a mosque where the king and the lord and the factory-owner are made jointly responsible for the elementary necessities of life of

---

9 ii. 268.
10 iii. 92.

the subject and the peasant and the wage earner. I shall just quote extracts from two verses:

Those who establish regular Prayer,
And give regular Charity,
And have (in their hearts)
The assurance of the Hereafter,
These are on(true) guidance
From their Lord; and these
Are the ones who will prosper.[11]

Or

But if they repent,
Establish regular prayers,
And practise regular charity,—
They are your brethren in faith.[12]

Whosoever wants to enter the brotherhood of Islam shall have to establish regular prayers and pay Zakāt regularly. It is obvious that those who want to remain in that brotherhood shall have to pray and pay Zakāt. Both the practices are equally fundamental in importance. Such distinguished followers of Islam as Abū Bakr and 'Umar agreed that they are equally important. Abū Bakr said, "By Allah! I shall fight those who make a difference between prayer and Zakāt for Zakāt is a tax on wealth. O Allah! If they withhold from me even a she-kid which they used to make over to the Prophet of Allah (peace and blessings of Allah be on him), I shall fight against them for their withholding it!" 'Umar said, "By Allah! Allah opened the heart of Abū Bakr (to receive the truth), so I know that it was true."[13]

Its Purpose

The purpose for which Zakāt is levied was made perfectly clear both by the Qur'ān and the Prophet. Says the Qur'ān:

Alms are for the poor
And the needy, and those
Employed to administer the (funds);
For those whose hearts
Have been (recently) reconciled
(To Truth); for those in bondage
And in the debt; in the Cause
Of God; and for the wayfarer;

---

11. xxxi. 4-5.
12. ix. 11.
13. Bukhārī: *Sahīh* 24 : 1.

(Thus is it) ordained by God,
And God is All-Knowing
And Wise.[14]

All jurists agree that "Alms" in the above verse refer to Zakāt because in this verse they are "ordained by God" and compulsory charity is Zakāt. Besides, one of the heads of expenditure prescribed is "those employed to administer the (funds)" showing that Zakāt shall be collected and expended on a national basis. Here six out of the eight heads on which Zakāt money can be spent are connected with poverty. The purpose of Zakāt therefore is to pay for: (1) the poor,[15] (2) the needy,[16] (3) whose hearts have been reconciled to truth,[17] (4) those in bondage,[18] (5) those in debt, and (6) The wayfarers.[19] The remaining two heads of expenditure are: (7) the remuneration of the functionaries who have to collect and expend Zakāt and (8) any other noble cause for which money may be needed: in times of emergency this should be taken to mean defence and in normal times propagation of the faith, because the former preserves and the latter seeks to establish the social system of Islam.

Zakāt is not the only source of national income to be wholly or primarily spent in rooting out poverty. Such another is *Fai* which means porperty abandoned by the enemy or taken from him without a formal war. Assigning items of expenditure of *Fai*, the Qur'ān explains the end that God has in view for the social system of Islam:

What God has bestowed
Of His Apostel (and taken
Away) from the people
Of the townships,—belongs
To God,—to His Apostle
And to kindred and orphans,

---

14. ix. 60.
15. The disabled person who, on account of some defect, is unable to earn his living.
16. Though fit to earn is unable to do so on account of poverty or lack of resources.
17. "Men who have been weaned from hostility to Truth, who would probably be persecuted by their former associates and require assitance until they establish new connections in their new environment."— A Yusuf Ali
18. "Those in bondage, literally and figuratively: captives of war must be redeemed; slaves should be helped to freedom; those in the bondage of ignorance and superstition or unfavourable environment should be helped to freedom to develop their own gifts."—A Yusuf Ali.
19. Strangers stranded on the way.

The needy and the wayfarer;
In order that wealth may not
Make a circuit (merely)
Between the wealthy among you.[20]

What God wants us to be careful about is that "wealth should not make circuit only among the wealthy". Zakāt also is to be levied and expended with the same end in view.

The principle of Zakāt is made clearer still by the Prophet in the instructions he gave to Mu'ādh when he sent him to Yeman. He was instructed: "Invite them to bear witness that there is no god save Allah, and that I am the messenger of Allah; if they accept this, tell them that Allah has made obligatory a charity in their wealth which is taken from the wealthy among them and *returned* to the poor among them."[21]

How eloquent is this word "returned"! This obligatory charity is charity only in the sense that it has a spiritual and moral connotation. Otherwise, what the wealthy are called upon to pay for the poor is what really belongs to the poor. The wealthy do not exclusively own the wealth that they possess. They share its ownership with the poor. At the end of every year the share of the poor is to be calculated and "returned" to them.

Its Special Contribution

Apart from the realisation of social justice, Zakāt makes special contribution which has absolutely no parallel in any other economic system, past or present. Zakāt is the uncompromising enemy of hoarding. Hoarded wealth is the first item on which Zakāt is assessed. Indeed, no secular system can possibly tackle the problem of hoarding with the effectiveness with which Islam can do, because hoarded wealth can be taxed only with the co-operation of the hoarders. And there is no reason why the hoarders should co-operate with the taxing authority against their own dear wealth. In Islam, on the other hand, the fear of God and the fear of the Day of Judgment are enough to force co-operation upon the hoarders against their wealth. It would be almost

20. lix. 7.
21. Bukhārī. 24 : 1

impossible for a Musalman not to unearth his hoarded wealth after reading this verse of the Qur'ān:

> And there are those
> Who bury gold and silver
> And spend it not in the Way
> Of God: announce unto them
> A most grievous penalty—
> On the Day when heat
> Will be produced out of
> That (wealth) in the fire
> Of Hell, and with it will be
> Branded their foreheads,
> Their flanks and their backs.
> —This is the (teasure) which ye
> Buried for yourselves: taste ye
> Then, the (treasures) ye buried![22]

Hoarding here includes not only gold and silver when they are buried in the earth, but *all wealth which is kept lying unused.*

According to Islam wealth should be used to perform two functions only, viz. it should either be spent on good things of life or invested in commerce and industry. To these two channels, Musalmans are repeatedly enjoined to direct their wealth. Mark the contrast from the ascetic religions of the world:

> O ye people !
> Eat of what is on earth
> Lawful and good;
> And do not follow
> The footsteps of the Evil One
> For he is to you
> An avowed enemy.[23]

And again:

> O ye who believe!
> Eat of the good things
> That We have provided for you,
> And be grateful to God
> If it is Him ye worship.[24]

Earning of wealth (which cannot generally be done without investment) is considered so important in Islam that the Qur'ān permits trade even in the course of pilgrimage:

---

22. ix. 34.
23. ii. 34.
24. ii. 172.

It is no crime in you
If you seek of the bounty
Of your Lord (during pilgrimage).[25]

And again:

And when the prayer
Is finished, then disperse
Ye through the land
And seek of the bounty
Of God.[26]

The special significance of Zakāt is that it is the avowed enemy of hoarding.[27] Islam suggests two alternative channels to which surplus wealth should be directed. Either spend that wealth on comforts of life or invest it in trade or industry. What happens when people spend money on good things of life? The demand for all kinds of consumption goods increases, and the industrialists and producers find an opportunity to extend their production. Trade becomes brisk and employment is extended. The result is that the nation becomes more prosperous. What happens when wealth is invested in industry and commerce? Employment increases and more of good things of life are produced. They even become cheaper enabling more men to purchase them. More human needs are satisfied and more men are employed. Again, the result is prosperity and welfare of the nation. Hoarding, however, has the opposite effect. To the extent that wealth is hoarded, it sets a limit to the extension of production; therefore to the extension of employment; therefore to the extension of national welfare and prosperity. In the economic domain, hoarders are the greatest criminals. Nor wonder, the Qur'ān has announced "unto them a most grievous penalty".

Conventional Basis of Assessment

The following are the forms of wealth on which conventional doctors of law generally consider the tax of Zakāt to be applicable.

(1) ***Hoarded Wealth:*** Besides accumulated wealth which lies unused for one year, it also includes excess of annual

25. ii. 198.
26. lxii. 10.
27. In this context hoarding means leaving surplus wealth idle.

earnings over annual expenditure, which is not invested in trade or industry, and remains lying with the owner for one year. If the owner is in debt, his debt is excluded from the taxable sum. There is, for each kind of wealth, a minimum exemption limit called *niṣāb*. In the case of silver the *niṣāb* is 200 dirhams or 52 ½ tolas (nearly 21 oz.) In the case of gold, it is 20 *mithqāls* or 7 ½ tolas (nearly 3 oz). In the case of ornaments, the *niṣāb* is that of silver if the ornaments are made of silver, and that of gold if the ornaments are made of gold. In the case of cereals the *niṣāb* is five *wasaq* "which according to two different calculations, comes to twenty-six maunds and ten seers, or eighteen maunds and thirty-five and a half seers, or nearly a ton in the first case, and about two-third of a ton in the second."[28] In the case of other forms of wealth, the *niṣāb* is judged by their value in silver.

After deducting *niṣāb* and debt, all idle wealth is taxed at the rate of 2 ½ %.

(2) Mines and Treasure-trove:

If a mine or a treasure-trove is discovered in the land of a Musalman, he is to surrender one-fifth of it to the State to meet needs of social justice. In the case of mines, Zakāt will take the form of taking away one-fifth of the income from the working of mines. It has been pointed out that under the present circumstances much more than one-fifth of mines is generally taken by the State. Sometimes entire mines are nationalised. The point here is that Islam enjoins that one fifth of mineral wealth, irrespective of whether they are owned by individuals or by the State, should form Zakāt revenue to be spent exclusively on the items mentioned in the Qur'ān.

(3) Tax on Agricultural Produce:

In the case of agricultural land which depends for irrigation on rain-water or natural springs, the tax is one-

28. M. Muhammad Ali. *The Religion of Islam*, p. 470. Explaining the difference, the learned author says, "The difference arises from the meaning of sa', which according to the people of Iraq, is eight *rati* in weight and according to the people of Hijaz, five and one-third *rati*."

tenth of the land produce. Where land is irrigated by wells or other artificial means in which labour is engaged by the owner, the tax is one-twentieth of the produce of land. Maulana Muhammad 'Ali, objecting to its inclusion in Zakāt, says that this "is not technically Zakāt, it is really land-revenue".[29] We need not fight about its name. We have to see the function that it performs. But if we call it land revenue or a portion thereof, in case an Islamic State decides to levy more than one-tenth on the produce of land, the essential point is the particular head of expenditure this income would cover. The jurists agree that one-tenth of the produce of land is to be taken by the State and spent in the cause of the poor. That is what makes it Zakāt even though it is revenue derived from land.

(4) Tax on Capital:

(a) Tax on herds of cattle. Herds of cattle are subject to a capital tax varying between 1% and 2 ½%.

The following rule is laid down for camels. "One goat for five camels, and, after that, one for each additional five or part of five, up to 24. When the number reached twenty-five, a she-camel, one year old, sufficed up to 34. From 35 to 45, the age was raised to two years, for 46 to 60, to three years; for 61 to 75, to four years. For 76 to 90, two young she-camels of the age of two years were given as Zakāt; for 91 to 214, two of the age of three years, and after that one she-camel of the age of two years for every forty camels, or one of the age of three years for every fifty camels was to be added."[30]

In the case of goats and sheep, Zakāt is one goat or sheep from 40 to 120, two for 121 to 200, three for 201 to 300 and after that one for each hundred or part of hundred.

29. Ibid., p. 471.
30. Ibid., quoted from Bukhārī, 24 : 38.

In the case of cows, a one-year old calf for every thirty cows and a two-year old one for every forty are prescribed.

Horses are taxable according to their value at 2 ½ %

(b) Tax on trade capital. Merchandise, in whatever form, is generally considered taxable at the rate of 2 ½ %. A *ḥadīth* reported by Dārāquṭnī and Ḥakam tells us that the Holy Prophet mentioned cloth for sale as one of the things on which Zakāt was payable. Dārāquṭni also reports that Caliph 'Umar ordered a certain man who traded in skins to pay Zakāt by having the price estimated. And there is a *ḥadīth* reported by Samura Ibn Jundab: "The Holy Prophet used to command us that we should pay Zakāt out of what we had for sale."[31]

Imām Bukhārī however, did not find any reliable *ḥadīth* supporting a tax on merchandise. Besides the question of the reliability of the *ḥadīth* quoted, they do not mention the rate of the tax or whether there is any exemption limit or not. The jurists, however, have assumed the tax ratio to be 2 ½ %.

Similarly, there is no *ḥadīth* to show whether capital tax levied on herds and merchandise is to be extended to industry and buildings that are rented. But if we accept the principle of capital tax, there is no reason why buildings and industry should be exempted.

To sum up, to meet the demands of social justice, Zakāt revenue is got from a levy of 2 ½ % on all idle wealth, one-tenth to one-twentieth of all agricultural produce, one-fifth of all mineral wealth, and a tax on the entire capital of the whole nation. There has been almost a consensus of opinion about these provisions. The last of these needs a little critical examination to which we shall proceed in a moment; but before we do so we shall see

31 Abū Wāwūd, Sunan, 9 : 31

what a modern critic of Islamic economic system has to say against Zakāt.

An Answer to Professor Smith

Professor Smith in his work, *Modern Islam in India*, has devoted one paragraph to Zakāt. Having assumed that Zakāt is only "an annual levy on the unused surplus assets of the possessing classes,"[32] he easily reaches the conclusion that "most states in the world have had something of the kind, though in modern states it is always something much more substantial." The deduction is left to the reader that since advanced capitalist countries, in spite of doing "something much more substantial," could not provide social security to the masses, how could poor Islam achieve it with its meagre 2 ½ % of "unused surplus assets"? We are informed that Zakāt is "distinctive in form only, not in principle"; and that it is "relevant to a predominantly agricultural society". He probably thought he was giving another argument against Zakāt by rounding of the discussion with: "No modern independent Islamic state had adopted it—Egypt, Turkey, Iraq, Iran, etc."

The last argument, if it can be called one, is just as relevant to a discussion on Zakāt as the statement: "A, B, C, and D who are suffering from malaria do not take quinine," would be relevant to a discussion on the efficacy of quinine as a remedy for malaria. Indeed, we ourselves would be off the track if we tried to explain the reasons and the circumstances which have kept these countries much too engaged with political problems to settle down the details of their economic policy.

Let us now turn to the other statements of the author which would have been perfect arguments if they corresponded to facts. But they just do not. To begin with, Islam does not only tax "the unused surplus assets of the possessing classes". As we have already seen, besides the idle wealth, it also taxes the entire agricultural produce, the entire mineral wealth and the entire capital of the nation which are, by far, much more substantial

32. W.C. Smith, *Modern Islam in India*, p. 100.

sources of revenue than the levy on the "unused surplus assets". We believe he was not intentionally misrepresenting Zakāt in order to establish that Islam "represents a stage in social development prior to" both capitalism and socialism. To make such statements means, to put the best interpretation on them, that the author just doesn't know what is Zakāt.

Having completely misunderstood Zakāt, it is not strange that the author adds: "Most states in the world have had something of the kind, though in modern states, it is always something much more substantial." How misleading the statement is when we know that Zakāt does not spare any form of national wealth: and Allah "ordains" that the Muslamans should not rest contented until poverty and need have been rooted out! It was indeed an astounding revolutionary concept at the time when the Qur'ān was revealed more than thirteen hundred years ago, and although the world has seen many changes since and heard much tall talk, it remains a revolutionary concept still when we note how definite minimum portions are assigned from agricultural wealth, mineral wealth, trade and industrial capital as well as idle wealth to meet the requirements of the poor and the needy. Which "modern state" has set aside a specific portion of the entire agricultural produce to meet social needs? Which "modern State" has set aside one-fifth of its mineral wealth for the cause of the poor? Which "modern State", has taxed the capital of trade and industry to provide social justice? And which "modern State" can possibly tax the idle and hoarded wealth in the absence of religious sanction? If no "modern State" has done anything of the type, how misleading and incorrect it is to say; "Most states in the world have had something of the kind, though in modern states it is always something much more substantial"!

It is similarly incorrect to say that Zakāt is "distinctive in form only, and in principle". It is a revolutionary concept to change all forms of national wealth for the purpose of social justice, to make rooting out of poverty the first duty of the State and above all to make it as important for every Musalman as prayer itself.

Lastly, Zakāt is not only "relevant to a predominantly agricultural society" but is also relevant today when communism is making experiment with millions of human lives; and will be relevant tomorrow when the spirit of man will rise in revolt and vanquish communism.

Zakāt for Today

In the context of today we should re-examine the provisions of Zakāt and see whether, in the case of any one of them, the Musalmans need to exercise their inherent right of *ijtihād*. It should be clearly understood that it is the principle of Zakāt which is fixed and unchangeable for all times, not so the details of the form. If at any time we find that the poverty of masses cannot be removed by the revenue of Zakāt assessed on conventional basis, there is nothing to check the Musalmans from increasing the ratio of the tax or changing its form. Indeed they, in that case, would be working absolutely according to the spirit of the Qur'ān. There is a *ḥadīth* which guides us to this conclusion.

Fāṭimah bin Qais[33] said: The Messenger of Allah (peace and blessings of Allah be on him) said: "In (one's) wealth there is a due besides Zakāt," then he recited:

It is not righteousness
That ye turn your faces
Towards East or West:
But it is righteousness
To believe in God
And the Last Day,
And the Angels
And the Books
And the Messengers,
To spend your substance
Out of love for Him,
For your kin,
For orphans,
For the needy,
For the wayfarer,
For those who ask,
And for the ransom of slaves;
To be steadfast in prayer,
And practise regular charity.

33. *Mishkāt*. 6. 6.

Allah says that forms are not important. Righteousness does not lie in turning our faces towards the East or West. The principles are important. We have to practise regular charity towards certain ends. Whatever the form which will suit the ends, we will adopt it. We will not fix our faces always towards the East or towards the West, but will follow the path which leads us to our goal--rooting out of poverty. This has been made clearer still by Ḥaḍrat 'Alī: "Allah has ordained that the rich are to pay out of their wealth *to that extent which is sufficient for the needs of the poor*; so that if they do not find food or clothing or they struggle (unsuccessfully for their living) it would be because the rich are not doing their duty, and Allah will take them to task on the Day of Judgment and will punish them."[34] So, that is the eternal principle of Zakāt: the rich are always to pay "to that extent which is sufficient for the needs of the poor".

The first item of Zakāt revenue, namely, a levy of 2 ½ %, on the idle wealth, need not be changed. The details about *ṇisāb* may be re-examined. This tax is not so much intended as a source of revenue as to whip wealth into action. This portion of Zakāt would probably always remain a distinctive feature of Islam's economic system, and would always operate in the direction of forcing wealth to come out of hoards and be invested in trade or industry, or increase the demands of goods. Either way it would increase employment in the country.

It would be relevant to inquire, in view of Islam's inability to countenance the Western theories of interest and also the banking structure that has been raised on the concept of interest, whether it would be required of us to tax bank deposits as idle wealth. We have already seen that the bank deposits are not always directed to productive channels and even when they are they vitiate the healthy growth of the economic system. Since taxation of idle wealth is the foremost objective of Zakāt, an Islamic State would be failing in its duty if it does not include bank deposits and other interest-bearing investments like preference shares in idle wealth on the same basis as gold and silver. This of course will retard the growth of banks as they exist now, and possibly lead to their

34. Muḥallā, Vol. VI. p. 158.

disintegration. This tax, therefore, would not be feasible so long as alterantive banking structure has not been devised. Lord Keynes considered Liquidity Preference as the bane of modern financial structure and went to the extent of suggesting that money should be made to bear a carrying cost so that it may be forced towards either spending or investment. His idea was that currency notes should bear the date of issue, and should be legal tender only for a fixed period and then additional stamps should need to be affixed to them periodically to make them legal tender. If this were practised the people who desire to keep their assets in a liquid form may yet find a way out by hoarding gold and silver which the burdened with no carrying costs. This system would therefore be cumbersome without being foolproof. As Keynes also emphasised the negative role of interest since it sets a limit to the marginal efficiency of capital, it may have been in his mind, with this institution of a carrying cost on money, to counteract the rate of interest on bank deposits. But even this purpose may not be served and banks may in fact raise the rate of interest to the extent of the carrying cost of money. We, however, have the clear direction of Zakāt to tax all idle wealth. If we interpret the first provision of Zakāt according to the requirements of modern times, we shall blaze a trail for a confounded world. But the application of this provision of Zakāt would need a new banking structure in which the reward of capital is not fixed but variable. After this has been done, we can tax all idle wealth including all interest-bearing bank deposits in such a way that if the rate of interest is correspondingly raised, the rate of tax may be found progressively heavier. If, as a result, the banking structure based on interest disintegrates, we will not need to shed a tear, as our alternative banking structure with variable capital return would be there to take its place.

The second and third items of Zakāt revenue, namely, a levy on agricultural produce and a levy on mineral wealth, should also remain. In their details, however, ijtihād may be exercised. The representative assembly of an Islamic State is competent to consider whether the rate of taxation should not be increased. An Islamic State today would charge considerably greater tax on land than one-tenth of the produce. Here again we shall need to interpret this provision of Zakāt according to the conditions that exist. The provinces of Pakistan already derive revenue from land without being specifically considered as Zakāt or being largely spent on the requirements of "the poor" and "the needy". Indeed little has been done so far to provide industrial homes for the able-bodied beggars or poor-houses for those who, due to some physical defect or deformity, are unable to earn their living. There are millions of landless labourers in Pakistan who have no permanent occupation to follow, and quite often no occupation at all. These are some of the first objects on which Zakāt revenues will need to be spent. The provinces at present impose land revenue and spend it on Law and Order, civil services, judiciary, roads and buildings, education and health. All these are essential items of expenditure. It is as impracticable to ask the provinces to forgo their land revenue so that objectives of Zakāt may be served, as it is to ask them to meet the requirements of "the poor" and "the needy" as completely as the Qur'ān demands, without curtailing any of the other provincial services. Clearly the purposes of Zakāt demand an additional taxation of land. The last settlement of land in which land revenue was fixed was made a long time back; in the Punjab, for instance, some fifty years ago. The land revenue was then determined at one-fourth of the rental value of land. Rental value was then explained as one-fourth of the share of the landlord. Assuming that the landlord receives one-half of the produce from the tenants, the government share works out at one-eighth of the harvest. The value of the harvest was then determined according to the price level of agricultural products. Since the time this tax was determined agricultural prices have risen almost four times. So that what the government now receives is really 1/32nd of the value of the harvest. It is no wonder that when the government charges three times the land revenue from the refugee peasants and six times the land revenue from local peasants who work on evacuee lands, the peasants are keen to have an allotment of land made in their favour at this level of taxation.

A reassessment of land revenue is obviously called for. Even without taking the needs of Zakāt into consideration, it would be done to increase the provincial revenues, on which the demands, among others, of health and education are becoming increasingly pressing. If in the new assessment land revenue is pitched considerably higher, as it is likely to be, it would be desirable to make it variable with the increase or fall of agricultural prices. However, even a new assessment, keeping in view the multifarious provincial needs, may not be able to make any provision or leave any room, in the present system of land tenure, for a fresh 5% tax on unirrigated land or 10% on irrigated ones. The requirements of Zakāt demand that we pitch our hopes on a reorganisation of agriculture itself. Our lands at present are not yielding all that they can. The landlord system, which has long outlived its utility, discounts the initiative of the peasants. Continuous subdivision of holdings and their fragmentation have excluded the possibility of any substantial improvement. The entire system of land tenure calls for a radical change, which should include the buying over of all landed interests which perform no work on land and only act as drones. They should be paid at a multiple of the rental value of land, and the tenants, who would become the future owners, should pay this price in instalments spread over a number of years. Once this is done it will become possible to increase the size of our sub-average and uneconomic holdings. Co-operative farming would then be able to show the way to twice or thrice the value of the present harvests. It would then be possible to impose Zakāt, in addition to the conventional land assessment. It should, therefore, be clear that a reorientation of our land policy and land tenure is as essential to the organisation of Zakāt as the fashioning of a new banking structure is a prerequisite for it.

For the proper functioning of Zakāt it would be necessary to create an authority charged with the collection of all Zakāt revenues and their proper disbursement according to the requirements of time. Both these taxes, viz., taxation of all idle wealth and the land tax, will be administered by it.

The third Zakāt tax, the one of 20% on mines, will involve financial readjustment. Some mines are nationalised, others are given on lease, still others pay a variable royalty. In the case of nationalised mines, 20% of the income should be given to the Zakāt Authority. Similarly, in the case of mines given on lease, 20% of lease money, and in the case of royalty mines a similar percentage of royalty money should be handed over to it.

There is, however, some confusion in the case of the fourth item, namely, capital-tax. The tax on herds of cattle is clearly stated but is relatively unimportant. Tax on merchandise is hinted in a few *aḥādith*, but they do not prescribe any measure of taxation. No mention is made of industrial capital, but it is obvious that the provisions of the tax on trade would extend to the sphere of industry Implements of artisans are specifically excluded, and this should mean the exclusion of modern plants and factories, but raw materials, for instance on orthodox reckoning, would still be taxable. Our jurists have generally held that all forms of capital are taxable at the rate of 2½%. If we apply this capital tax today in an Islamic State, it will gravely retard the growth and extension of industry and trade. Its effect would be just the opposite of the abolition of interest. With the abolition of interest a modern Islamic State was expected to remove the brake which does not let the wheels of commerce and industry to function freely. We will remove that brake but substitute another and even more effective one, because its incidence would be wider, by levying a capital-tax. Just as we tax the produce of land and not the land itself it is even more necessary that we should tax the income from trade and industry and not merchandise or factories. Levying a capital-tax on trade and industry instead of a steeply graduated income-tax would be like killing the goose which lays the golden egg, because the growth of the capital wealth of the country would be checked, and there is every risk that capital wealth may even decrease which would mean unemployment, reduction of purchasing power and therefore further curtailment of production. In fact, we would defeat the very purpose for which we wish to apply capital-tax, namely, national welfare.

There are a few practical difficulties also in its execution in the context of today. Supposing the Islamic State which levies Zakāt in the form of capital-tax has non-Muslim minorites. Obviously, the State would tax only Muslim capital because it would be objectionable to force the non-Muslims to pay Zakāt. This would mean that Muslim trade and industry would be handicapped in an Islamic State! The Islamic State would be forcing the Muslims to pass on their trade and industry to the non-Muslims. This certainly would be contrary to the best interests of Islam.

Now let us suppose that there is no non-Muslim minority in our hypothetical Islamic State. In that case the Islamic State would handicap its entire trade and industry in comparison with other countries of the world which do not levy a similar capital-tax. This would amount to the Islamic State's suppressing its own trade and industry and encouraging trade and industry of foreign countries in the world market.

In one case alone it is feasible to impose capital-tax on industry. If a plant or industry in workable condition remains unworked for one year, capital-tax should be imposed on it and should be treated as hoarded wealth.

It is possible that in the circumstances of tomorrow which we cannot at present foresee, it may become necessary to impose capital-tax on trade and industry to provide revenue for social requirements. In that eventuality there would be nothing to check us from returning to the conventional basis of assessment. However, we shall not speculate about tomorrow, because here we are concerned only with Islam's economic order for today. In the conditions obtaining in the Islamic lands today, when industry and trade need all the encouragement and support which the governments can give them, it would be highly injurious to the prosperity of the peoples to impose a tax on the capital employed in industry and trade.

The author sent a questionnaire on this point to a few learned *'ulamā* in this subcontinent. Only two of them sent their replies. Both of them agree that income and not capital of trade and industry should be taxed. Maulānā Muḥammad 'Alī of Lahore refers to his views expressed in his book—*The Religion of Islam:*

> Machinery employed in industry should follow the same rule. It should, in fact, be rgarded in the same light as the implements of an artisan, and its earnings become taxable when the necessary conditions as to the assessment of Zakāt are fulfilled, Stock-in-trade should be treated in a similar manner; that is to say, only the yearly profit should be taxable, not the stock itself.[35]

Maulānā Abul Kalām Āzād writes:

> Certainly its [Zakāt's] form shall be that of income-tax.
>
> The real orders in this respect are the verses [in the Qur'ān] relating to Zakāt. No form of ratio has been prescribed by them. They only emphasise that the State should spend a portion of its income to meet the needs of the poor. The Prophet (peace and blessings of God be upon him) prescribed different ratios on different occasions. During the time of the first Caliph, the companions [of the Holy Prophet] thought over this problem and fixed the present ratio. This ratio is not obligatory but is subject to *ijtihād*. It is the duty of those who hold power that they should fix the proper ratio according to the economic conditions and needs of society in every age.[36]

It is for the representative assembly of the Muṣalmans to consider all the relevant factors and exercise *ijtihād* to substitute steeply graduated income-tax on trade and industry with an exemption limit instead of the capital-tax. Should it be so decided, we shall find that in countries where income-tax is already levied, as in Pakistan, we cannot duplicate it by imposing a Zakāt tax as well on trade and industrial profits. All that we can do is to leave this tax to the government that is at present administering this tax. A suitable allocation out of this tax be made by the government to the Zakāt Authority. There is after all no duality of the taxes of Church and the taxes of State in Islam just as there is none betweeen the spiritual and the temporal spheres. If a State is Islamic, is functioning to serve the cause of Allah by building a social structure according to the spirit of Islam, all taxes levied by it have the same spiritual sanction behind them as Zakāt itself. If we still suggest that Zakāt should be separately collected and administered by an Authority created for this purpose we do so for two reasons. Zakāt takes idle wealth, including idle factories

35. *The Religion of Islam*, p. 427.
36. Translated from an Urdu letter of Maulānā Abul Kalām Āzād addressed to the author.

and interest-bearing loans. This is completely a novel form of taxation and yet, from the social point of view, it is of the highest vlaue. There is no reason why the social system should forgo this income. The second argument in favour of Zakāt being separately administered is that the Zakāt Authority would be able to concentrate on those of the items of expenditure provided in the Qur'ān which have not received adequate attention at the hands of the governments. The very first provision provided by the Qur'ān is for the poor and the needy. It should, therefore, be difficult to call a country Islamic which has any beggars roaming about its streets. The problem of unemployment calls for an undivided attention, and this will be given to it by the Zakāt Authority, which shall have its own funds with which to implement its decisions and yet its activities will be complementary in nature to the functions of an Islamic government.

To sum up, Zakāt should be levied on (a) all idle wealth, which includes gold and silver and jewellery (in the conventional assessment jewellery is excluded and appears unjustified), idle cash (which will include current deposits), all interest-bearing loans, hoarded corn and cornered consumption goods, provided they have remained in this condition for one year; (b) 20% of income, royalties or lease moneys of all mines; (c) 10 % of the value of land produce from unirrigated tracts and 5 % from irrigated ones; (d) an allocation from the income-tax receipts of the government.

It was this conception of *ijtihād*, always capable of unfolding new meanings in the eternal principles of Islam, which Iqbal had in his mind when he said:

New foliage would its principles put on,
Eternal though, it would new shapes assume,
No shift would ever shatter it within,
Without it would for ever be renewed.[37]

37. Dr. Sir Muhammad Iqbal, *Jāvīd Nāmah*, p. 74.

Chapter 5

The Fascist Fiasco

The Rise of Fascism. The Programme of National Socialism. Marxist Verdict on Fascism. Marxist Verdict Examined. Fascism and `Marxism Compared. Total Planning and Liberty. Islam and Fascism Contrasted.

The Rise of Fascism

Fascism officially dates from March 1919 when Benito Mussolini founded the first *Fascio de Combattiments* in Milan. The word Fascio means bundle or bunch and referred to the close union and organisation of the adherents of the movement.

Although the movement began in Italy, it attained its logical perfection in Germany, and our examination will mainly concern itself with the latter country. Except that the two movements were based, broadly speaking, on similar principles and strove towards similar ends, there was no other link between them. They started independently of each other in response to the urge to make their respective countries great. The two movements may have even fought each other if the foreign affairs had taken a different shape and either movement had found it more conducive to national interests.

In Italy an armed Fascist *squadron* was formed which mostly comprised of ex-combatants who had been made desperate by the sight of their country, victorious in the First Great War, but failing to come to its own on account of the factious minority of socialists. The capitalists helped it as it held out promise of protection to them against the socialists, and the labourers voted for it as it promised to end unemployment. The vast majority of adherents were also inspired by patriotism as the fascists had decided that Italy must "reaffirm her right to complete historic and geographic unity and fulfil her mission as the bulwark of Latin civilisation in the Mediterranean".[1]

The conditions which led to National Socialism in Germany were much more desperate. At the end of the First Great War, she found that her agriculture had deteriorated, her industry was disorganised, her greatly reduced manpower was in a state of physical exhaustion, and her population had suffered greatly in health and standard of living. On top of it came the realisation that her currency, due to war measures, had greatly inflated. At the beginning of the war currency circulation was estimated at 6 billion marks—comprised of 2 billion worth Reichsbank currency and 4 billion worth gold coins and token currency. Thereafter, gold coins were replaced by paper currency, which, at the end of war, stood at 28.4 billion marks: a 1400% increase compared to paper currency in the beginning of the war. The obvious need was gradual deflation and steady reconstruction, but it was made impossible by the terms of the armistice and the peace treaty.

The economic terms of the armistice were that:

> Germany should deliver, 5,000 railway engines, 150,000 freight cars, the whole of the railway in the Alsace of Lorrain and 5,000 more trucks and should return all the gold taken from the banks of the conquered countries; and should accept the continuation of blockade until the Peace Treatry was signed; and in addition pay, because Germany was alleged to be guilty of causing the war, reparations which were to be fixed by the Peace Treaty.[2]

The Peace Treaty signed on 28 June 1919 provided:

> Allied occupation was to continue until 1935.....Alsace and Lorrain were to be ceded to France as also the Saar coal mines: the Saar province was to be administered by the League of Nations for 15 years and then its return was to be determined by a plebiscite; certain parts of Germany adjoining Belgium were to be given to her....; upper part of Schleswing was to be given to Denmark; parts of West Prussia, Posen and upper Silesia were to be given to Poland; Danzig was to be

1. *Encyclopaedia Britannica*, article "Fascism".
2. Professor Savkar, *Modern Economic Development of Great Powers. pp. 353-54*

made a free city under the administration of the League; Memel was to be internationalized; East Prussia was to be separated from the West by a corridor to be given to Poland to give her an outlet to sea; colonies were to be divided among the Allies as mandated areas; France was to be given 38 million tons of coal per year for ten years, also many chemicals and livestock for the destruction suffered by her; Germany was to bear the cost of the Allied army of occupation and the various commissions set up to enforce the terms of the Treaty; Germany was also to grant the most-favoured-nation treatment to the Allies in her trade though they were not bound to give her the same treatment.[3]

In addition Germany was to pay as reparations 132 milliard gold marks.

All these terms, particularly the reparations, promised to make Germany's economic reconstruction almost impossible. The Social Democrats, who had assumed power after the revoltion of 1918, tried to do their best in a very bad job. Their first task was to check currency inflation. But as they had come to power with labourers' votes and depended on their support, they were compelled to implement their election promises of higher wages and salaries and greater social security. As the government could not meet this extra burden from its budget, this meant further inflation.

Reparation payments could be made if Germany had corresponding foreign trade-surplus in her favour. But the war and the treaty terms had reduced her agricultural output and she needed to import food and raw material for her industries, with the result that she could not gain the necessary favourable trade balance. She sold her foreign assets as well as transferred gold from the Reichsbank. This being insufficient, she had to sell paper marks to foreign buyers. This led to the depreciation of the mark. "The pre-war ratio between the dollar and the mark was 1 : 4; when exchange operations were resumed in January 1919, the rate had dropped to 8, in December it was 50; in 1920 it varied between 40 and 90, in 1921 between 60 and 250."[4]

It was obvious that Germany was heading towards a crisis if the burden of reparations was not removed. Accordingly, the German government asked for two years' moratorium. Though the

3. Ibid., pp. 354-55.
4. Ibid., p. 357.

request was very genuine, it was turned down. The German government had no alternative except to print money to pay reparations. As inflation set in, German capital migrated to foreign countries; and people rushed to buy things fearing further inflation. The result was that the Mark became almost worthless. Lord d'Abernon estimates that in the final stages of the great inflation £ 1 was equal to 43,000,000,000 Marks.

The result was that the people faced starvation and there was great danger of the spread of Bolshevism. The working capital of German industry was wiped out and it was difficult to get fresh credit. To stabilise the currency a new unit of currency, Rentenmark, was introduced. One Rentenmark was made equal to 1,000,000,000 old Marks. The stabilisation was a success as the government ruthlessly cut down its expenditure. The government gained by this measure as it wiped out its entire war debt. But industry and trade suffered a grave loss; and the rentier class was reduced to proletariat, providing a very fertile ground for the spread of National Socialist movement, which all along had emphasised that Germany simply could not pay reparations and it was madness to follow a "policy of fulfilment" and which now pointed to the collapse of the currency as a vindication of its policy and programme.

A commission under Dawes was sent to inquire into the ways and means by which Germany could pay the reparations. The Dawes Plan was the result of their investigations. They recommended payment of reparations by Germany in the form of gruaduated instalments beginning with a small volume. They suggested organisation of internal taxation under the supervision and control of foreign powers to enable Germany to meet the obligations under the Peace Treaty. The Dawes Plan, by its reorganisation of finance and taxation, increased the credit of German government and industry in the foreign market, and provided premises for the recovery of German industry. But, as the execution of the plan entailed foreign control of German domestic affairs, it provided yet another opportunity to National Socialists to make their voice more impressive for the average German patriot. Germany, they cried out, is losing her sovereignty by "a policy of fulfilment"; and they prophesied further strangling of German economy on account of the rush of foreign borrowing both by German government and German industry and trade. The Allies' failure to realise that Germany simply could not pay the huge sum of reparations gave birth to Fascism in Germany, and their bungling of the problem from year to year marked the growth of the Nazi cult from strength to strength.

Between 1924 and 1929 German government as well as German industry continued to borrow abroad: the former to pay the reparations and the latter to reconstruct itself as well as it could. But it soon became clear that Germany's foreign indebtedness was assuming alarming proportions. National Socialist outcry against foreign control of German economy also had its effect. The Allies in 1929 made a new arrangement with Germany, which came to be known as the Young Plan. By it financial autonomy was restored to Germany and the annual payment of reparations was reduced and spread over fifty-nine years (till 1988).

With redoubled energy the National Socialists tried to win power to stop this long-term strangling of Germany's economic system. They issued their twenty-five points embracing all aspects of national life, and waited for the next crisis which was round the corner to have the reins of government in their hands.

The Young Plan, even as a measure of relief, had come a little too late. The slump had started. Interest rates were rising and having their adverse effect on industry. While German industry was already nervous, crash occurred on the New York stock exchange. It put a stop to the flow of capital to Germany, and instead a withdrawal of foreign funds started on an alarming scale. The nervousness of foreign creditors developed into a panic with the collapse of Credit Instalt, one of the biggest Austrian banks, in 1931. The Reichsbank increased the rate of discount but the withdrawals showed no signs of abatement. To save the banks from impending collapse, the government closed them indefinitely on 14 July, 1931. The banks were reopened and a standstill agreement was signed between Germany and her foreign creditor banks. But the loss of credit had already impaired German economic structure, and world-wide depression also had its repercussion. A quick succession of governments followed which could only inadequately tackle the problem. So, in 1933, the German people decided to give the twenty-five points of National Socialism a trial.

The humiliating Peace Treaty, particularly efforts at extorting the impossible reparations, was the main current which brought the upsurge of National Socialism. Our discussion of the social implications of National Socialism will gain in clarity if we consider one more tributary that fell into that main current. It was the revolt of the German youth against cramping and unconstructive Western civilisation. It began in 1913 with the Manifesto of Free German Youth which said: "We determine to fashion our lives in obedience to our own conscience, accepting the burden of our responsibility; we are determined to maintain this freedom under all circumstances." It was a revolt against the social systems which are decayed, and sought freshness of life in excursions in the countryside, in wearing simple clothes, in leading hard lives, and in building up strong bodies. The movement was national for they selected the centenary of the rise of Germany youth against Napoleon for the assertion of their cultural freedom. Otto Zarek points out that "to be a member of the Wandervoegel did not remain a passion of a few queer people, of strange and perhaps abnormal youths. The movement quickly gained adherents all over the country, mostly high-school boys, and soon counted a hundred thousand members. It is not in spite of but because of the platonic intimacy among the members that this sect became a pattern for the Nazi groups that came later. The revival of old German rites and songs and especially the attention which the movement lavished on the peasants entitle one to say, justly I think, that it was one of the intellectual heralds of Nazism."[5]

Soon came the disillusion and the suffering and the economic collapse of the post-war decade which we have already seen with the result that the movement gained in adherents and embraced

---

5. Otto Zarek, *German Odyssey*, p. 38.

millions. It soon became "coextensive with the youth of the entire nation" so much so "that no adult body, party or church, not even the Catholic, could hope to hold youths unless it provided them with, or permitted them to adopt, a tolerable imitation of the pagan Wandervoegel".[6]

The vast numbers who joined this movement are an index of the revolt of the German youth against the materialistic and scholastic standards, a measure of the widespread mysticism which sought life in an emotional contact with the soil "so that the National Socialist destruction of scholarship must have appeared to them merely as confirmation of convictions intuitively arrived at. Why should the burning of books concern a generation that sought reality on top of a mountain?"[7]

The primitive and barbarous aspects of Nazism were heralded in this movement. Hartshorne quotes from the autobiography of a Berlin boy who was in the movement between 1918 and 1923:

> Mysticism and everything mystical had dominion over us. It was in our ranks that the word *Fuehrer* originated, with its meaning of blind obedience and devotion. The word *Bund* arose with us too, with its mysterious of conspiracy.[8]

It was the German youth who sought something new and thrilling in social environment. National Socialism appeared to them to give it. And *Die Tat*, the organ of the Wandervoegel, became the first intellectual defender of Hitlerism.

The Programme of National Socialism

The salient features of the National Socialist programme were:

(1) It was opposed to liberalism. It considered essential that programme of the party should be carried out implicitly and the orders given by the party leader should be obeyed without demur, "for nothing is more dangerous to the existence and the striking

---

6. Leslie Paul, *The Annihilation of Man*, p. 101.
7. Ibid., p. 102.
8. E.V. Hartshorne, *German Youth and the Nazi Dream of Victory*, p. 12.

force of a movement such as ours than the subjection of its principles to negative criticism and discussion."[9]

It was natural that democracy and democratic traditions should have been frowned at:

> It is clear that the law must evolve new concepts of public law to accord with innumerable innovations; that the scandal of the democratic parliamentary vote will have to be removed.[10]

Autocracy was considered the most suitable form of government. "The form of State most suited to the German character is sovereign control concentrated in a supreme head."[11]

To remove all chances of liberal education ever subjecting the movement to critical examination, the school, the radio, and the newspaper were to operate under strict censorship and control. The prisnciples of the "suppression of all evil influences in the press, in literature, on the stage, in the arts and in the picture theatre"[12] were adopted.

Those who would show any signs of opposition to totalitarian methods had the threat hanging on their heads of losing German nationality:

> People who, even though German-born, act consciously in a way injurious to the nation and the state, and receive and obey orders from abroad, do not belong to the German community or destiny, and therefore cannot exercise the right of citizenship, any more than a Jew can do so, and there are many to whom we shall have to deny the high honour of enjoying these rights.[13]

(2) It was opposed to capitalism. Capitalism permits all individuals to seek their gain, and it presumes that the whole community would gain by this arrangement. Fascism does not leave things to chance. The claims of the community and the State are to have precedence over the claims of individuals. Each individual is to work for the good of the community; the result would be the gain of all individuals.

High finance and interest which are the basis of capitalism are rejected by Fascism. Hitler writes:

---

9. Gottfried Feder. *Hitler's Official Programme*, p.10.
10. Ibid., pp. 62-3.
11. Ibid., p. 69.
12. Ibid., p. 68.
13. Ibid., pp. 81-2.

> When I listened to Gottfried Feder's first lecture on breaking down the thraldom of interest in June 1919, I knew at once that here we had a theoretic truth which will be of immense importance for the future of the German nation...The campaign against international loans and finance has become the chief point in the programme for the German nation's struggle for independence and liberty.[14]

Unlimited amassing of wealth is opposed: "The welfare of the nation demands that a limit shall be set to the immoderate amassing of wealth in the hands of individuals."[15]

Monopolies which are concerned only with profits and have scant regard for communal good are to be nationalised: "Big business (syndicates, trusts) will be nationalised.[16]

(3) Fascism is opposed to Marxism. Marxism envisages nationalisation of all poperty. National Socialism, on the other hand, considers private property necessary as an incentive for work. "National Socialism recognises private property on principle and places it under the protection of the state—provided that it is acquired and employed honourably."[17]

Fascism also rejects the fundamental premises of Marxism, namely, class-struggle. According to Fascism the conception of class is an extension of capitalistic individualism. Instead of seeking the gain of one man against all other men, the gain of one class is sought against all other classes. Fascism lumps together both capitalism and Marxism and rejects them both:

> Capitalism and Marxism are one! They grow on the same intellectual base. There is a whole world of difference between them and us, their bitterest opponents. Our whole conception of the construction of society differs from theirs. It is neither a class-struggle nor class selfishness; our supreme law is the general welfare.[18]

According to Fascism, the interest of workers and employers is the same, namely, national welfare. Trade unions which seek only the advancement of one class were therefore abolished. To protect the labourers, labour legislation was passed. Regulation of National Labour (1934) provided:

(a) Mutual Trust Councils to be formed, with the employer as leader and two to ten labourers as members, to increase the

---

14. *Mein Kampf*, Vol. I, pp. 244-5.
15. Gottfried Feder, op cit., p. 89.
16. Ibid., p. 91.
17. Ibid., p. 88.
18. Ibid., p. 101.

efficiency of workers, to settle disputes and to frame and apply work regulations.

(b) The government-appointed Labour Trustees to settle the disputes which could not be settled in the Mutual Trust Councils. Their decision was final.

(c) All concerns employing more than twenty persons were to issue work regulations showing working hours, wages, schedules for determining piece-work wages,grounds on which employment could be terminated without remuneration.

(d) Every worker was to do his best for the good of the concern, as well as for the good of fellow-labourers. Anyone found lax in his duty was to be dealt with by the Courts of Social Honour.

Fascism does not denounce all employers. If they keep their prices low while maintaining the quality, pay their employees well, always look to improvements in plant, they are praised and regarded as great assets for the economic life of the community.

(4) Fascism seeks total planning. Fascism is the revolt against the conflict of individuals and classes. All such conflicts, according to Fascism, arise on account of the lack of planning which breeds disorder, chaos and conflict. This develops hatred and disintegration of national life. In Fascism all things are planned. Everybody is expected to work for the national welfare and the good of all individuals is expected to result therefrom. In Fascism wages are fixed, prices are fixed, production and distribution of all things are planned, the school is controlled as well as the press, the radio, the currency, the finance the parliament and hosts of other things important in individual and national life. No opposition is brooked, for opposition means conflict, and conflict on hypothesis breeds out of the absence of planning. No discussion is to be tolerated, because discussion shows weakness of planning and uncertainty about the ideal. "The great task which National Socialism has set before it is a determination to restore form, to dispel the chaos, to set the disjointed world in order again."[19] Therefore total planning complete regimentation of life.

(5) Fascism stands for aggressive nationalism. It should be noted that Fascism eschews differences and conflicts only within a

19. Ibid, p. 51.

national territory. All efforts at planning are directed towards the progress of the national State as against the whole world; the uplift of one people as against all other peoples. "It is the axiomatic right of every self-conscious nation that it should strive to include all the members of its race in a closed national state....consequently we do not surrender a single German who lives beyond the frontier of the German state and within the frontiers of another civilised state or colony, as regards his national membership with the German Reich."[20] In the beginning it was emphasised that it does not mean imperalistic tendency; but with rise to power on the basis of total planning it was necessary that the Fascist State should try to grab whatever it thought to be its own, by force of arms. Strife and conflict are to be ended within the State to conserve the power to do so beyond its frontiers.

(6) Fascism believes in racial superiority of its adherents. To place its otherwise unaccountable aggressive nationalism on a rational basis Fascism inculcates belief among its adherents that racially they are superior to the whole world. Since there is something inherently superior in one race against all other races it is natural that the former should have more industry and commerce and land and other good things of life than other races have. Hence the justification for aggression.

In Germany, this concept of the superiority of the German race was raised to an academic level. The school dinned it into the ears of the impressionable young, and the press convinced the older generation, and learned theses were written on the subject. The whole nation came to believe in it. It is noteworthy how, in the absence of discussion and criticism, the best educated nation came to believe in one of the most stupid theories of this century. Can the Russians be blamed if they believe with equal conviction an equally stupid theory, viz., class-struggle?

Fascism in Germany singled out the Jews as the focus of animosity of their nation against all other nations. If Nordics are the most superior race, the Jews are the most inferior. Even the Jews who have the purest Nordic blood are no exception. They all

---

20. Ibid., p. 76.

deserve to be robbed, killed, humiliated and exterminated. "Anyone who sees in the Jews merely 'German citizens of the Jewish religion'—and not an alien, sharply segregated people, strongly parasitic in character—will fail to appreciate the essential nature of this demand (exclusion of Jews). If a man were to say or think that a cabbage which had grown by chance in the middle of a strawberry bed was a strawberry plant and that good strawberries could be got from it, he would be as wrong as if he thought that a lion cub which had got in among a flock of sheep had thereby become a sheep."[21]

Marxist Verdict on Fascism

It is interesting to note the Marxist view of Fascism. Marxism, wearing as it is the coloured glasses of class-struggle, is forced to consider Fascism as "capitalist reaction". Marxism is forced to assign Fascism some place in the material processes of history. In Marxism things can either be "progressive" —if they lead to the "dictatorship of the proletariat,"—or "reactionary"—if they retard or hinder that supreme realisation. Fascism refuses to assign any value to the concept of classs; in fact, it seeks to abolish them; therefore Marxism considers it "reaction"; and since reaction can proceed only from the possessing and capitalist classes, therefore Marxism can most confidently dub it as "capitalist reaction".

Marxism explains that due to the strain of the First World War capitalism had met a crisis. The masses were bound to end capitalism altogether and embrace Marxism, but capitalists, realising the danger, gave financial help to National Socialists in order to keep capitalism in the saddle.

It is pointed out that German capitalism being a later product always needed State protection. This new capitalism had to bear the burden of the great war suffered defeat, lost colonies and territories, and therefore raw materials and markets. On it fell the additional burden of reparations. It was now ripe for collapse in favour of the "dictatorship of the proletariat". World capitalism

21. Ibid., p. 78.

had to do all it possibly could to check this possibility. They poured loans into the German economic arteries lest it should collapse. Besides, the victors kept a huge occupation army more to check any uprising of the left than to perform the routine duties of a conquering army. German capitalism realised the need of the hour, and made a friendly gesture to foreign capitalism in the shape of Weimer Republic by which it promised to discard the militarist past of Germany, and in return sought the help of credit from foreign capitalism. German capitalism knew that it would mean foreign inroads into her monopolies, but this was preferable to total extinction at the hands of the Marxists. Thus it was an arrangement of mutual help by the two capitalisms: German capitalism forgoing a part of her spoils in return for foreign capitalism's saving it from total collapse.

The mutual help continued for some time until the slump set in. Exports began to shrink and profits began to contract. Foreign capitalism found it no longer profitable to give more credit to Germany; they instead began to withdraw capital, leaving German capitalism to face the situation independently. How could it face the situation independently except by pulling down the internal standard of living? But the masses under democratic institutions would not allow this. So the democratic institutions must go. Weimer Republic should yield place to Fascism.

In Fascism capitalism appeared in a new garb. It did not identify with the reactionary figures whom the masses knew. It skilfully chose a leader from the masses, exploited national sentiments, pointed out the failures and weaknesses of democracy, attracted to itself labourers by promises it could never fulfil; all sorts of dreamers, cranks and schemers joined it; and by intense propaganda it made itself popular enough with all classes to sweep the polls. As soon as Fascism came to the helm, the standard of living could be pulled down and German capitalism could continue to have its desired volume of profit. Thus it is that Fascism is "capitalist reaction".

Marxist Verdict Examined

Marxist explanation of Fascism is of a piece with Marxist method of sorting out the aspects and details which by clever presentation appear to confirm its theory of class-struggle. It conveniently overlooks, underestimates or distorts the facts that go against its thesis. Marxism cannot afford to tell the whole truth because it would tear to pieces the entire fabric of Marxism. We have seen what great contribution was made to Fascism by the German youth and their temper, but Marxism does not refer to it. We have seen that one of the fundamentals of Fascism is its opposition to high finance, monopolies and interest which are the life-blood and in fact the very being of capitalism. But this is an inconvenient fact: so overlook or distort it. Fascism is "capitalist reaction"; why should it nationalise big business? Why should it unequivocally state: "The welfare of the nation demands that a limit shall be set to the immoderate amassing of wealth in the hands of individuals"?[22] Why should it seek to break down the "thraldom of interest"?

Fascism denied freedom to all its adherents. All classes suffered from this suppression of freedom. But if we pick out a class on which the impact of this suppression was greater than on others, it is the capitalist class. Because capital needs free space to expand and exploit; and Fascism denies free space. This is how Hitler himself explained his policy:

> Each activity and each need of the individual will thereby be regulated by the party as the representative of the general good. There will be no licence, no free space, in which the individual belongs to himself. This is socialism—not such trifles as the private possession of the means of production: Of what importance is that if I range men firmly within a discipline they cannot escape? Let them then own land or factories as much as they please. The decisive factor is that the state, through the party, is supreme over them, regardless whether they are owners or workers.[23]

It must be a strange "capitalist reaction" that makes capitalists wear the tight jacket!

The fact is that National Socialism was not primarily concerned with economics, not to speak of its being pro-capitalist. Fascism in Germany was primarily concerned with politics: with building up an aggressive national State. Hitler has made it clear. "My party comrades, I am not thinking in the first instance of

---

22. Ibid., p. 91.
23. Rauchning, *Hitler Speaks*, p. 190.

economic matters. Certainly we need the wheat, the oil and the ores of these countries. But our true object is to set up our rule for all time, and to anchor it so firmly that it will stand for a thousand years."[24] Hilter was not following Marshall or Ricardo or Adam Smith; he only sought to out-Chengiz Chengiz Khan.

This subservience of economics to politics is clear in National Socialism's attempts at autarky. Germany needs to import food and raw material and export finished products to pay for the imports.National Socialism sought to make Germany as self-suffcient as possible. Now this arrangement is most uneconomic. Substitutes and synthetic products have to be invented at great cost and people are forced to consume them at higher prices than those of the cheap foreign products. This raises the prices and the exported articles, in case they cannot compete in the foreign market, have to be dumped or sold below their cost in order to get foreign currencies necessary for essential imports. This uneconomic policy could not have been dictated by capitalism. It was dictated by political policy and military considerations.

The racial policy of Fascism on which so much emphasis was laid was, if anything, anti-capitalist. Jews, broadly speaking, are the most acquisitive and capitalistic of people. Jews as representatives of capitalism became the worst victims of Fascism. Rationalisation of anti-Semitism was always attempted from this angle:

> The main battle is one between two world philosophies, represented by two essentially different intellectual structures —the active and creative spirit and the labile, acquisitive spirit. The creative spirit rooted to earth, yet overcoming the world in supersensual experience, finds its chief representative in the Aryan man; the acquisitive, rootless, commercial, materialistic spirit, aiming solely at worldy success, finds its chief representatives among the Jews.[25]

If capitalism was disguised in the form of Fascism it should not have robbed and exterminated the Jews for it would amount to suicide. "Seldom can a victorious ruling class have begun its career by an act of cannibalism."[26]

24. Ibid., p. 48.
25. Gottfried Feder, op. cit., p. 71.
26. Leslie Paul, op. cit., p. 67.

Fascist attitude to capitalists and capitalism explodes the Marxist verdict of Fascism. Let us see the problem from another angle. What is Fascism's attitude towards the proletariat and the proletariat's attitude towards it? If there is any truth in the Marxist verdict, Fascism must suppress the proletariat and the proletariat must abhor it. But we find that it is the proletariat whose votes helped Fascism to rise to power. The story of German revolution of 1918 and its failure to Bolshevise Germany makes a strange reading. The workers continuously support the Social Democractic government against the radical insurrections. The radicals insist that the Social Democratic have sabotaged the revolution. What is the workers' reaction? They support the social democrats! "The March strikes and street fighting in Berlin, the April strikes in Essen, Bremen and the Ruhr, the revolt in Brunswick, the Halle march of Weimar—a torrent of activity which should have led straight from the German February to the German October, yet did not. Through all, the German masses remained steadfast to the Republic. The working men most of all."[27] This was in 1919. The communists continued their efforts for fourteen years to convert the workers to their side during which there occurred two major crises of capitalism for them to exploit. But the workers kept up their support of the Social Democrats until they shifted their sympathies to Hitler. Workers could not have been so very insensible about their gain to continue to vote for Social Democrats if they were really the enemies of the proletariat. Similarly, if Fascism was "capitalist reaction," why should the workers have voted it to power against the communists? "At the height of depression, which was to make Hitler Chancellor, the German branch of the party of the historic November revolution could poll no more than 15 per cent of the total votes."[28]

Nor did the Fascists suppress or exploit the workers. We have already seen the details of Regulation of National Labour (1934) which protects the rights of the workers. When Nazis came to power, eight million people were unemployed; in 1945

27. Ibid., p. 76.
28. Ibid.

there was felt a shortage of labour in Germany! Is this really "capitalist reaction" to provide employment to the unemployed? Nor does the extension of insurance schemes for the workers by the Fascists reveal their "reaction".

The National Socialists continued all the four insurance schemes (insurance against accident, insurance against sickness old-age insurance, unemployment insurance) with certain modifications regarding benefits and their duration. In 1934 an Act was passed to consolidate all the systems. To supplement the social insurance benefits in certain cases, they started a voluntary organization known as the Nationalist Socialist Welfare Association (M. S. V.). Its activities consist of: care of mother and child, child welfare, unemployment assistance, war victim relief and care of the rentier, aged and infirm. It has the largest membership of any relief organization in the world: in 1935 it was 4,700,000. The organization maintains 13,000 creches and 500,000 beds.[29]

Is this really "capitalist reaction"?

There is a reason why, in spite of the overhwelming evidence, Marxism should insist that Fascism is "capitalist reaction". Fascism, of course, is not workers' revolution. In Marxist terminology, therefore, it can only be "capitalist reaction," because in the historical struggle between the classes no third phenomenon is possible. If a third phenomenon occurs, Marxism is forced to make it appear "revolution" or "reaction". If Fascism is neither of these— "neither capitalist reaction, nor workers' revolution, there is no place for it in the Marxist categories. To admit this is to admit either that the class-motivation of history has suddenly and unaccountably broken down, or that the premises of the Marxist theory of history are false. To remain Marxist one must therefore strenuously, and if necessary against all the facts, assert the identity of Fascism and capitalist reaction."[30]

Fascism and Marxism Compared

We have seen that Marxism is at great pains to establish that Fascism is akin to capitalism. It is interesting to note that Fascism brings the same charge against Marxism. "Capitalism and

29. Savkar, op. cit., p. 349.
30. Leslie Paul, op. cit., p. 71.

Marxism are one! They grow on the same intellectual base. There is a whole world of difference between them and us, their bitterest opponents. Our whole conception of the construction of society differs from theirs. It is neither class-struggle nor class-selfishness; our supreme law is the general welfare."[31] So the first common factor among them is that they consider each other capitalistic. And the second is that the accusation of each is equally preposterous. Neither Fascism nor Marxism is capitalistic. They are both revolts against the waste and exploitation of capitalism. They are both revolts against poverty in the midst of plenty that capitalism permits. One insists that it is the proletariat that must rise as a class and take hold of all instruments of production. The other considers imposition of strict control on all aspects of economic life essential for a healthy economic structure.

Both of them are opposed to liberal traditions and democratic institutions. One insists that "dictatorship of the proletariat" is essential to end exploitation: the other considers the vesting of sovereignty in an individual by the party necessary for ruthless elimination of all waste. Both of them maintain the facade of representative government while taking away the substance of it. No opposition party is recognised. All opposition, whether organised or individual, is put down as being in the pay of the foreign enemies. Both depend for the maintenance of their power on the secret police and the concentration camps. Both exercise stringent control on the press, the radio and the theatre. Both give lopsided education in the schools. Dialectical materialism is the central part of curriculum in the Russain schools, just as the doctrine of the superiority of the Nordics and the inferiority of the Jews formed the most essential education in the German schools.

Both of them are indifferent towards religion, at times they are even hostile to it. "God created man in His own image" is something which both of them fail to appreciate. They do not consider individual life sacred. The inviolable sanctity of human life is reduced to a farce when men are not free to move about as they like, to think what they prefer, to believe what they consider

31. Gottfried. Feder, op. cit., p. 101.

the truth, to express what they believe to be right. Both of them force men to barter away their freedom for a loaf of bread. Both of them fill the belly of man. Both of them take way his soul.

However, belly of man they do fill. Both of them accomplish material advancement. Both of them root out poverty and unemployment. They lift up the underdog, provide social security, build hospitals, sanitoria and maintain creches. Both of them harness Nature for the benefit of man. They build huge dams and great factories and produce as many good things of life as possible for the average man and woman. They achieve these great and difficult things. But in each case they are attained at a terrible cost: too big a cost for even these great things. However, each refuses to recognise the achievements made by the other!

Their outlook does not embrace all men. Each works for a class or race and robs and kills the other classes and other races. They strive to provide benefits to one set of men as against all the rest. Similar motives dictate the fight against the exploiters and the Jews.

> The function of anti-Semitism in the political system and the mass propaganda of Nazism is perfectly plain. The Jew is substituted for the bourgeois, just as the race-conscious nationalist has taken the place of the class-conscious proletarian. Both political systems demand the raising of a conflict of interests into the absoluteness of a myth. Both need a correlate for their centre of salvation in the visible form of a spirit of evil.[32]

Total Planning and Liberty

Though Fascism has been defeated in the Second World War, and is in the course of being obliterated in Germany and Italy, it should not lull anyone into a false sense of security. The danger to human liberty from Fascism is only less than that from Marxism. Fascism is likely to raise its head in the most unexpected quarters. It is possible for the best of men, who attach the greatest amount of sanctity to individual liberty, to work unconsciously for Fascism. They will think they are only working against waste and exploitation, and only pleading for a planned economy. Order, they will say, is so obviously better than

---

32. Hermann Rauschning *The Beast from the Abyss*, p. 155.

disorder. And most men whose intentions are better than their critical faculties will agree. What would be the result? Planning would begin. Well, nothing wrong there. But planning is something which is not satisfied until everything in all its aspects to the last detail is covered by the plan. From planning would proceed total planning, perfect order. Therfore no friction. Therefore no discussion, no criticism. The colossal plan has got to be executed for the good of the masses. It needs Herculean efforts for execution. Discussion and criticism weaken the spirit of execution, produce doubts, entail delay. They should therefore be suppressed. Therefore control the press, control the radio, control the school, put limits to the free association of men. Now the very men who voted for planning will see the web in which they are caught. They will try to come out of it but they cannot. If they utter a word against the system they will be accused of being in the pay of the vested interests. The secret police will be necessary to segregate all such men in concentration camps without wasting time about the formalities of law. So Fascism would set in. The danger of Fascism is in direct proportion to the temptation of total planning. Humanity can forget the great lesson that Fascism has taught us at its own peril. *There should always be drawn a definite line beyond which planning shall not go.* More and more men need to understand what Louis Fischer has already understood:

> To jump from the monism of uncontrolled capitalism to the monism of uncontrolled state ownership, or state domination, of all property, industry and finance is no solution. In fact, it is highly dangerous. Even in countries where there is a stronger tradition of democracy and personal freedom than in Russia and Germany, the omnipotent state—omnipotent because it owned and (or) ran everything—might still become a menace to liberty....
>
> I am opposed to putting the entire economic life of a national community into the hands of property-owners and bankers who must use their wealth primarily to earn wealth for themselves. But I am no less opposed to giving the whole job to governments. Society today needs an economy of checks and balances, one in which the state can check private capital, in which private capital can balance the state, and in which citizens organised as consumers, or as producers with little or no property, can check and balance both the state and capital.[33]

---

33. Louis Fischer, *Men and Politics*, pp. 624-25.

Herman Rauchning in his books on Fascism has done a signal service to humanity in pointing out the great temptation for total planning and therefore the great lurking danger from it:

> This tendency to systematic completion as a total, absolute machinery of rule with a precise technique and procedure in the exercise of power, lies, in the nature of the state as developed in the seventeenth century. All that Bolshevism and Fascism are doing through their conception of the state is to develop the totality of the exercise, of power in a new way under the new conditions determined by technical porgress and the rise of the masses. This development is taking place of necessity wherever a modern machinery of power is formed to exercise according to a general plan the central leadership by a social group of every expression of life. Hence every form of total mobilisation, every system of preparation for war, and every system of political and economic planning on a grand scale is exposed to the risk of developing into a form of the new state or an absolute community or a partial absolutism. The characteristic final result of this development is the identity of absolute state and totalitarian community.[34]

Total planning is a euphism for making everyone toe the line.

Islam and Fascism Contrasted

The fundamental difference between Islam and Fascism in the economic field is that Islam is opposed to total planning. Islam seeks the expansion of production not by taking into its own hands or under its rigid control all instruments of production, but by removing the fundamental brake to the expansion of production, namely, interest. Fascism also seeks to abolish "the thraldom of interest". But in Fascism the promise was not kept. Fascism issued government bills bearing 4½ % interest. This is not the way to abolish "the thraldom of interest". But Islam means what it says. It is opposed to interest, all forms of interest.

Subject to this one limitation it permits the economic system to function freely. It goads everyone to earn his living and raises it to the level of a religious duty. Man is asked to go about and harness the forces of Nature to his advantage:

> It is God Who hath created
> The heavens and the earth
> And sendeth down rain
> From the skies,and with it
> Bringeth out fruits wherewith

---

34. Herman Rauschning, *The Beast from the Abyss*, p. 114.

To feed you; it is He
Who hath made the ships subject
To you, that they may sail
Through the sea by His command;
And the rivers (also)
He hath made subject to you.
And He hath made subject
To you the sun and the moon,
Both diligently pursuing
Their courses; and the Night
And the Day hath He (also)
Made subject to you.[35]

All that is in Nature is subjected to man, for him to exploit for his benefit. But all the time Islam is aware that there would be many people who, on account of some inherent defect, would not be able to earn their livelihood, and there may be many others whom the economic system may fail to absorb and who may be unemployed or under-employed. Islam, therefore, comes to take away one-tenth of all agricultural produce, one-fifth of all mineral wealth, and a steep progressive income-tax or capital-tax which may be sufficient to provide necessities of life to all who are poor or needy. Islam calls these taxes Zakāt, and raises them to the level of prayer in importance.

This is not to say that there is anything in Islam against planning. Islam only lays great stress on the sanctity of the individual. Islam does not agree that men can be killed for the benefit of the nation. In the literature of the world there is nothing that can compare with that verse of the Qur'ān which emphasises the sanctity of the individual life:

That if anyone slew
A person—unless it be
For murder or for spreading
Mischief in the land—
It would be as if
He slew the whole people.
And if anyone saved a life,
It would be as if he saved
The life of the whole people.[36]

So planning in Islam cannot go beyond the limit where free space has to be denied to the individual.

35. The Qur'ān, xiv. 32-33.
36. v. 32-33.

Islam expressly stands for democratic institutions. Some of the essential qualifications of the Musalmans are:

> Those who hearken
> To their Lord, and establish
> Regular prayer, and who (conduct)
> Their affairs by mutual consultation.[37]

There are no supermen in Islam who can forgo the necessity of criticism and discussion. Even the Prophet is ordered to consult other men in all affairs:

> And consult them
> In affairs.[38]

When affairs can be conducted only by mutual consent and consultation, there cannot by any occasion of an imposed order, no gagging of men, no regimentation of life, no secret police, no concentration camp, no censorship and control of the press and platform, the radio and the school.

And, finally, Islam does not uphold one class or one race against other classes or races. Men, according to Islam, are a single nation: "Mankind was not single nation."[39] No territorial, racial or class superiority or inferiority is recognised. Men, as such, are all equal. The affairs of all are in the hands of their Lord Who will judge them on the Day of Judgment. White and black, Jew and German, bourgeois and proletarian, Muslim and non-Muslim, will have equally to undergo His strict scrutiny and are capable equally of winning His Grace:

> Those who believe (in the Qur'ān)
> And those who follow the Jewish (scriptures)
> And the Christians and the Sabians,
> *Any* who belive in God
> And the Last Day,
> And work righteousness
> Shall have their reward
> With their Lord; on them
> Shall be no fear; nor shall they grieve.[40]

37. xlii. 38.
38. iii. 159.
39. iii. 213.
40. ii.62.

Chapter 6

Inheritance And Miscellaneous

Islamic Law of Inheritance. Its Economic Implications. Death Duty. Miscellaneous.

Islamic Law of Inheritance

It is not our purpose here to give at length the provisions of the Islamic law of inheritance worked out with over-elaboration by our jurists. From sect to sect and school to school there is a great amount of hair-splitting which is generally as unimportant as it is uninteresting.

We shall rather turn to the Qur'an which has clearly laid down the principles of inheritance:

God (thus) directs you
As regards your children's
(Inheritance): to the male
A portion equal to that
Of two females: if only
Daughters, two or more
Their share is two-thirds
Of the inheritance;
If only one, her share
Is a half.
For parents, a sixth share
Of the inheritance of each,

If the deceased left children;
If no children, and the parents
Are the (only) heirs, the mother
Has a third; if the deceased
Left brothers (or sisters)
The mother has a sixth;
(The distribution in all cases
Is) after the payment
Of legacies and debts...
In what your wives leave,
Your share is a half,
If they leave no child;
But if they leave a child,
Ye get a fourth; after payment
Of legacies and debts.
In what ye leave,
Their share is a fourth,
If ye leave no child;
But if ye leave a child,
They get an eighth, after payment
Of legacies and debts.
If a man or a woman
Whose inheritance is in question
Has left neither ascendants nor descendants
But has left a brother
Or a sister, each one of the two
Gets a sixth; but if more
Than two, they share in a third;
After payment of legacies
And debts.[1]
God directs (thus)
About those who leave
No descendants or ascendants
As heirs. If it is a man
That dies, leaving a sister
But not child, she shall
Have half the inheritance:
If (such a deceased was)
A woman, who left no child,
Her brother takes her inheritance;
If there are two sisters,
They shall have two-thirds
Of the inheritance
(Between them): if there are
Brothers and sisters, (they share),
The male having twice
The share of the female.[2]

1. iv.11-12.
2. iv. 176.

A few more principles of inheritance are derived from the *Ḥadīth*. A man in his lifetime has absolute power to spend or dispose of his property as he likes. Nor is his right detracted by any distinction between acquired and inherited wealth. But he cannot make a legacy about it beyond one-third. The *Ḥadīth* gives the reason.

> Bequeath one-third and one-third is much, for if thou leavest thy heirs free from want, it is better than that thou leavest them in want, begging of (other) people.[3]

Thus legacy made even for charitable objects cannot exceed one-third. No legacy is to be made in favour of one of the sharers, reducing or increasing the share of any of his relatives:

> Surely Allah has given to everyone entitled to anything his due, therefore there shall be no bequest for one who inherits.[4]

If after giving the assigned shares to inheritors something is left it is given to the nearest made:

> Give the appointed portions to those entitled to them. Then whatever remains is for the nearest male.[5]

Thus shorn of sectarian differences and hair-splitting of jurists Islamic law of inheritance is this: After paying off the debts of the deceased and legacies which donot exceed one-third of what he has left and are not made in favour of any of his inheritors, his property will be divided so that the shares of the parents and husband or wife shall be taken out first.

The parents will get one-sixth each, if the deceased has children. If the deceased has no issue nor brothers or sisters, the mother takes one-third, the remaining two-thirds go to the father. If the deceased has no issue but has brothers or sisters, the mother gets one-sixth. "It is not here stated what the father shall get and what the brother's and sister's share shall be. The prevalent view is that the presence of brothers reduces only the mother's share; the remaining five-sixth going to the father."[6]

The husband gets one-half if the deceased has no issue, and one-fourth otherwise. The wife gets one-fourth if the deceased has no issue and one-eighth otherwise.

---

3. Bukhārī, *Ṣaḥīḥ*, 23 : 36.
4. *Mishkāt*, 12 : 20
5. Bukhārī, *Ṣaḥīḥ*, 85 : 4.
6. M. Muḥammad Ali, *The Religion of Islam*, pp. 706-70.

After paying off the shares of parents and husband or wife, the rest of the property goes to the children, the son having double the share of the daughter. If there are no children and there is a brother or a sister one-sixth goes to him or her; if he has brothers and sisters one-third would go to them, brothers getting double the share of sisters.

If the deceased leaves neither children nor parents, the whole of the property, after the husband's or the wife's share has been taken out, shall go to brothers and sisters; if there is a single female, daughter or sister, she shall take one-half of the property, a single brother following the same rule; if there are two or more daughters or sisters they shall take two-thirds, the residue going to the nearest male according to Ḥadīth; if a person entitled to inheritance is dead but leaves behind offspring, that offspring shall take his place; if the father or the mother is dead, the grandfather or the grandmother shall take his or her place;....if there are no brothers or sisters, the nearest relatives after them, such as father's brothers or father's sisters, shall take their place.[7]

Its Economic Implications

The primary contribution of the Islamic law of inheritance to the economic structure of its society is that it runs counter to the concentration of wealth in a few hands. The moneyed man during his life is denied unearned increments by the abolition of interest. He is goaded to enter creative occupations like industry or trade. On his income he has to pay Zakāt whose incidence would be proportionate to the requirements of social security. Besides the obligatory charity he is urged to give charity in the way of Allah. If he has still amassed wealth or has built up large property, it will not be concentrated in a single hand after his death. Islam recommends him to make a will for charitable objects which shall not exceed one-third of the whole estate; and the remainder shall be shared by almost all the relatives. So that the huge estate which had been built up during the lifetime of a person is reduced to tiny portions. The inheritors might again, by their industry, build up fortunes for themselves in spite of the heavy Zakāt duty, but when

7. Ibid., p. 709.

they die, their fortunes will again be fragmented among their relatives, males as well as females. Compare it to some other systems of inheritance which permit a person to give away his wealth to a single child to the exclusion of all others and that child can amass and build up still greater fortune till in the course of a few enterprising generations a colossal estate is built up. The result is something like the Mitsui in Japan who own 12½ % of the entire national wealth while millions in Japan have to live on subsistence wages.

Islam considers this fragmentation so important that it takes away the right of the owner to reduce or enlarge the shares which are assigned by the Qur'ān. During his life he has every right over his wealth, whether inherited or acquired. He can spend it, make a gift of it, or do whatever he likes with it. But he can make no will about the property which will enlarge the share of one of his inheritors even by a penny against the other shares.

In India this law of inheritance was largely circumscribed and made ineffective by the British Government which gave greater weight to custom than to provisions of the Islamic law. With the establishment of Pakistan, these customs are being gradually superseded by Islamic laws.

There are some critics who hold that the working of this law reduces agricultural land to uneconomic holdings. But the difficulty can be easily overcome by co-operative farming. If a person leaves five acres of land and seven sons, instead of dividing the land into seven shares, the seven sons can own the whole land, can plough it, and share the produce. Even if they divide the land, they can still join to cultivate it. Indeed the future of our peasantry lies in co-operative farming. No great improvement can be effected in our agriculture until the average size of holdings remains as small as it is today. If the peasants were educated, they could be made to understand that they should pull down several of their boundaries, join their neighbours in the cultivation of the whole land and share the produce according to the area that each possesses. Thus four peasants owning 1, 2, 4, and 7 acres can join and divide the produce in the proportion of 1/14, 2,/14, 4/14 and 7/14, respectively. The purpose of the Islamic law of inheritance is to help the growth of the economic processes, not to retard or block them. If a man leaves a sugar mill and five sons, Islam does not ask them to break the plant into five portions but to own it joinly and share the profits. All that it provides against is that one son should not own the sugar mill to the exclusion of the other four.

This is not to deny the fact that in the matter of land co-operative farming gives only a short-term answer to the problem of fragmentation of holdings. Once the boundaries between the tiny patches of land are pulled down to bring out all that land is capable of yielding, the sharing of produce on the basis of ownership deeds will be challenged with increasing vehemence by men who quicken the dead earth to life. These are the boundaries that buttress the titledeeds, and provide a visible symbol of ownership. Once they cease to be visible and are replaced by the beautiful patterns which a strong plough can draw over an extensive field, even though it may be done only in the name of co-operative farming, all those demands on the harvest will be discounted which are unrelated to the actual performance on land. "The alternative is forced upon us either accepting the present concept of ownership of land, with all its consequences of fragmentation of holdings and obsolete agricultural methods, or relate ownership itself to the labour performed on land. There is yet a world to be won by the Musalmans if they realise the full implications of that famous *Ḥadīth* of the Holy Prophet in which he declared: "The land belongs to him who enlivens the dead earth."

The second economic implication is that, by providing shares for the daughters, sisters, mother and wife, it makes women active participants in the economic activities. One-half of humanity are not chattels who have no financial standing of their own. Nor are they drudges to be confined in the four walls of the house. They can own and possess, enter professions and services, join industry or trade and enter into contracts in their own names. Whatever they earn or inherit is their own and they are not obliged to give it away to anyone. If they are married, and Islam strongly recommends them to marry, their husbands are responsible for their livelihood as well as for that of their children. Islam has kept an essential difference in the obligations of man and woman keeping an eye on the physical disabilities of the latter. Whereas man has to earn for himself, his wife, his children and other dependants, woman's earnings are for herself alone. Of course, she can help her husband in the maintenance of the family but she is not obliged to do so. It was on account of this difference in the respective responsibilities of the two that Islam assigns men double the share of women. Critics who wish to give men and women equal shares forget that equality of unequals is inequality. It will be cruel to woman if we give her equal share along with man and make her share with her husband the responsibility for the maintenance of their families and dependants because the physical disabilities of the latter would not permit her to meet her obligations. It would be equally cruel to man if we make him responsible for the maintenance of the entire family and then do not relieve his burden by giving him double the share of a woman. In Islam a woman can earn and possess but she is not obliged to support anybody; a man can similarly earn and possess but he is obliged to support his wife, children and other dependants. The inequality of the burden is equalised by giving the man double the share of the woman in the matter of inheritance.

What is important here from the economic point of view is that in Islam woman has an identity of her own. She can spare her time and can enter into any profession or trade and thus increase the national wealth. Thus the whole man and woman-power is harnessed to prodce value, increase national wealth and add to human happiness.

That the Musalmans do not give to woman her due place, that they imprison her in the four walls of the house, not to speak of permitting her to enter commerce or profession, they send her out of home, even for social contacts, covered by a thick black veil, are as futile arguments against Islam as to say that Muslim landlords generally seek to give their estates to their eldest sons in contravention of the Islamic law of inheritance. During its decay Islam absorbed these foreign influences which during its renaissance it is determined to squeeze out.

Death Duty

Due to great demands made on a modern State for social security, universal provision of education and medical aid, it is possible that in certain exigencies a modern Islamic State may not be able to meet them exclusively from her great Zakāt revenue. Generally, there is no reason why this should be so. Because, as we have already seen, the sources of Zakāt are so great and the tax is so elastic that it can be easily expected to meet all the various demands of social security. But let us suppose a hypothetical case in which a modern Islamic State finds Zakāt revenue insufficient for essential services. What is to be done in that case? It would be reasonable in that case to seek further revenue by levying death duty. We have seen that the Islamic law of inheritance permits a man to give away up to one-third of his porperty for charitable objects. The Qur'ān (ii. 180) and *Ḥadīth* (Bukhārī, 55 : 1) make it the duty of a Musalman to write his will. We already how that the shares of all the heirs are fixed and the testator has no power to detract from or add to the shares fixed by the Qur'ān. What then can be the purpose of ordering him to write his will? The only reasonable explanation can be that he is ordered to make a will about one-third or less of his property which he has the power to give to persons other than his heirs. And what cause can be dearer to a Musalman than the cause of Allah for which he should provide in preference to his own kith and kin? So, the purpose of the Qur'ān and the *Ḥadīth*, referred to above, is to enjoin the Musalmans to provide for charitable objects anything up to one-third of their property in their wills. Whether he gives one-third or on tenth is left to his discretion. But something he *must* give.

The obligatory nature of making some provision in one's property for charitable objects can be made use of by an Islamic State. If there are exigencies in which demands of social justice or, in the language of the Qur'ān, "the cause of Allah," cannot be adequately served by Zakāt revenue, the Islamic law of inheritance will permit the State to levy death duty, which can extend up to one-third of all property left by its nationals. There can be no objection on the score of making compulsory and fixed what has been left by Islam flexibe, although compulsory enough. The Musalmans, as vicegerents of God on earth, have every right to pass any legislation which would further "the cause of Allah". They can fix any ratio of death duty for themselves so long as it does not exceed one-third, beyond which the Prophet forbids them to go.

Miscellaneous

Some of the miscellaneous provisions of Islam encouraging productive occupations and regulating them on the basis of fair dealing and generosity may be summarised here.

One of the fundamental principles of Islam in the economic sphere is that it tries to remove all blocks and brakes that retard production. Abolition of interest is the most significant contribution towards that end. The second contribution is this worldly attitude of Islam. Salvation of the spirit lies in living a worldly life on the basis of justice and good conduct. Worldly occupations are not to be shunned. They are recommended again and again both in the Qur'ān and the *Ḥadīth*:

> And when the prayer
> Is finished, then disperse
> Ye through the land
> And seek of the bounty
> Of God.[8]

And the Prophet said:

> Earning of lawful livelihood is a duty only next in importance to the duty (of prayer).[9]

And again:

> When you finish your morning prayer, do not sleep until you strive for your livelihood.[10]

Agriculture, industry and commerce are recommended as the finest professions. The Prophet said:

> There is no Muslim who plants a tree or cultivates land, then a bird or a man or an animal eats thereof, but it is charity for him.[11]

---

8. lxii. 10.
9. *Kanz-ul-'Ummāl*, Vol. II. quoted in Muḥammad Ḥifẓ-ur-Raḥmān, *Islām ka Iqtiṣādi Nizam*, p. 62.
10. Ibid., p. 63.
11. Bukhārī. *Ṣaḥiḥ*. 41 : 1.

Shaikh Badr-ud-Dīn 'Ainī, commenting on this *Ḥadīth* writes:

We are here told that one who plants a tree or cultivates land does charity even though he may not intend to do so. So that if a man plants a tree and sells it away or cultivates land and sells the produce, he will have done charity because by his efforts he has increased the livelihood of God's creation.[12]

Trade is even more strongly recommended. The Prophet said:

The truthful, honest merchant is with the Prophets and the truthful ones and the martyrs.[13]

In Islamic terminology no higher rank is possible. Earning by one's labour or by industry is equally good.

Says the Prophet:

No man eats better food than the one who eats out of the work of his hands.[14]

When asked about the best form of earning livelihood the Prophet replied, "Handicrafts."[15]

In fact all productive occupations are encouraged. Both men and women are eligible for all lawful occupations they may like to undertake and they have absolute right over the fruits of their labours.

And in no wise covet
Those things in which God
Hath bestowed His gifts
More freely on some of you
Than on others: to men
Is allotted what they earn
And to women what they earn:
But ask God of His Bounty,
For God hath full knowledge
Of all things.[16]

They are to earn wealth, but not to inculcate greed and acquisitiveness represented by interest. They should on the other hand do charity and be generous, for

God will deprive
Usury of all blessing,

12. 'Ainī's *Sharh-i-Bukhārī*. Vol. V, p 711.
13. Tirmidhi, 12 : 4.
14. Bukhārī. 34 : 15.
15. Ibn Mājah quoted by Muḥammad Ḥifẓ-ur-Raḥmān, op. cit., p. 250.
16. iv. 32.

But will give increase
For deeds of charity.[17]

Duty to Allah is more important than anything else. Therefore they are prohibited certain occupations:

Allah and His Messenger have forbidden trade in wine and the dead (animals) and swine and idols.[18]

Hoarding in order to gain high profits is also prohibited.

Whoever witholds cereals that they may become scarce and dear is a sinner.[19]

Lotteries and races and other forms of gambling are prohibited. So is the dealing in futures or satta: "The Prophet of Allah forbade me to sell a thing which is not in my possession at the time of selling."[20]

In dealings there should be no deception:
Give full measure when ye
Measure, and weigh
With a balance that is straight;
That is the most fitting
And the most advantageous
In the final determination.[21]

And says the Prophet:

The buyer and the seller have the option (of cancelling the contract) as long as they have not separated, then if they both speak the truth and make manifest (all relevant things), their transaction shall be blessed, and if they conceal and tell lies, the blessing of their transaction shall be obliterated.[22]

Employees should be properly treated and their welfare guarded:

It is the duty of employers to take only such work from their employees which they can easily do. They should not be made to labour so that their health is impaired.[23]

They should be paid proper wages:

Allah says there are three persons whose adversary in dispute I shall be on the Day of Resurrection: a person who makes a promise in My name, then acts unfaithfully, and a person who sells a free person and devours his price, and a person who employs a servant and

---

17. ii 276.
18. Bukhārī. *Ṣaḥīḥ*. 34 : 112.
19. *Mishkāt*. 12 : 8.
20. Quoted in Muḥammad Ḥifẓ-ur-Raḥmān. op. cit. p. 243.
21. The Qur'ān. xvii. 35.
22. Bukhārī. *Ṣaḥīḥ*. 34 : 19
23. Ibn Ḥazm. *Muḥallā*, quoted in Ḥifẓ-ur-Raḥmān. op. cit., p. 295.

receives fully the labour due from him and then does not pay the remuneration.[24]

Wages should be promplty paid:

The Prophet of Allah (peace and blessings of Allah be on him) said, "Pay the labourer before his sweat is dry."[25]

The labourer should also do his job to the best of his ability:

The Prophet of Allah (peace and blessings of Allah be on him) said, "The best earning is that of the labourer provided he does his job with care and regard for his employer."[26]

And finally all men (and women) in their transactions should develop a generous disposition:

The Prophet of Allah (peace and blessings of Allah be on him) said, "May Allah have mercy on the man who is generous when he buys and when he sells and when he demands (his due)."[27]

24. Bukhārī. 34 : 106.
25. Ibn Mājah quoted in Ḥifẓ-ur-Raḥmān, op. cit., p. 295.
26. Ibid., p. 297.
27. Bukhārī. 34 : 16.

Chapter 7

Islamic Banking

Finance for Public Works, Finance for Industry and Commerce. Insurance. Finance for Agriculture and Cottage Industries. Credit for Consumptional Purposes. A Word on Planning Pakistan and Islamic Banking.

Finance For Public Works

There is only one problem left for us to examine. Is Islam's economic system, after the abolition of interest, capable of devising some basis of credit for the various economic needs of a modern community? We shall consider all the different demands made for credit and see how we can substitute the inhuman and unproductive basis of interest by something human and productive.

As the Musalmans wrest complete independence in their lands, the most important economic problem for their States would be the need for credit for their programmes of construction like railways and basic heavy industries, irrigation and hydro-electric power. From where would the credit come to finance these schemes sponsored by a modern Muslim State? The present system in capitalist countries is that the governments get loans on fixed rates of interest from their nationals or from abroad, finance their schemes and go on paying interest on the capital invested. But we cannot accept this arrangement. We cannot squander government revenue badly needed for social services on the payment of interest.

There can be two more arrangements for getting this finance which would be perfectly valid according to Islam:

(1) Supposing the Muslim State needs credit to dig canals to provide irrigation facilities. The easiest course for it would be to borrow money on the basis of sharing the income from the canals. One-third of the water-tax might go to the lenders; one-third may be the additional revenue of the State; and one-third might be used to pay off the capital borrowed so that ultimately the entire income from the water-tax of those canals would go to the State. The State in this arrangement, without spending anything of its own, comes to possess a great source of revenue which is also a source of increasing employment and enriching peasantry. The State's revenue would also increase indirectly on account of the increase in the yield of lands. This arrangement is simply an extension of the principle of *shirākat*. i.e. co-operation, which is recognised by Islamic jurists.

Indeed all capital requirements of a modern Islamic State can be met with in this way. Railways and hydro-electric works, canals, large iron and steel works and shipyards and similar other works can all be built up without borrowing a penny on interest. All these works will bring in profits which the capital invested on them will share with the government. If national investments be not enough, foreign investments can be invited. In this arrangement the millstone of interest will not hang round the neck of the government finance. Capital will share the profits and share the risks. Parts of the increased revenue will form a sinking fund so that ultimately all these things become the property of the nation. Thus they are not only built completely free but provide a great increase in national revenue.

(2) There are things which cannot be built by borrowing capital in this way because they bring forth no profits or at least no profits which can be specifically determined. Roads are one such thing. How are we to get finance to build them? Let us read a page from Gottfried Feder which gives us the clue to the answer

According to him, the view that today great economic enterprises cannot be set on foot without recourse to loans is sheer lunacy. Here a reasonable exercise of the State's right to create money might produce the most beneficial results.

It must be clear to anyone that—for instance—a great hydro-electric plant might be erected in the following unexceptional manner:

The government introduces a bill in the legislature for exploiting the water-power of Bavaria, Saxony, etc. due regard being given to all economic requirements. The local Diet, or other body, decides on the construction, and empowers finance minister or the State Bank to issue a series of bank notes, marked specially to show that they are fully covered by the new works under contemplation. These notes are covered by the combined credit of the state and the Reich. No one can make any objection on the score of inflation. Construction is carried out on the additional credit granted by the council representing the nation, and the notes become legal tender like the rest.

When the work is completed, nitrates or electricity are supplied to customers against this money, and in a few years the issue can be recalled and destroyed. Result: the state,the nation, has instituted a new work, which secures to it a great new source of revenue, and the nation is the richer by it.[1]

Feder says, why should State borrow money for capital outlay? It can print it! But there is one difficulty to which Feder Joes not refer. When the quantity of money increases and other things remain the same, the value of money falls down and things become dear in price. If, however, the production of goods is speeded up to the proportion to which new money is needed for capital investment, there is absolutely no harm in printing money for capital outlay. Once when money is thus printed with proper precautions increase of goods on account of the State investments would in fact tend to bring down prices. This arrangement is by one means very novel. A great proportion of finance for fighting wars is generally secured in this way. If billions of notes can be printed to wage war against another nation, why can't one-tenth of them be printed to wage war against squalor and privation? The prices rise during a war because a major portion of production is divierted to the prosecution of war, the civilians are left with very few goods to purchase and the printing of money has got to go ahead without being able to give the necessary attention to price

1. Gottfried Feder, *Hilter's Official Programme*, pp. 94-5.

level. Within proper limits if money is thus created for productive works along with a nation-wide effort to produce more goods, there is nothing to prevent a modern State from avoiding to carry the millstone of interest round its neck. In the Bombay Plan this arrangement is adopted; and Rs. 3400 crores out of the total requirements of Rs.10,000 crores are proposed to be met with in this way.

Thus capital requirements of a modern Islamic State can be secured by borrowing money on the basis of sharing the profits arising therefrom. Equally important things for which finance is necessary, but do not promise to yield profits which can be easily determined, can be built with the help of created money.

Finance for Industry and Commerce

Here again two arrangements are possible by the application of the Islamic principle of *shirākat*:

(1) Joint-stock companies, by issuing ordinary shares, work on the same principle. It is only when they issue debentures—in which the return of the share-holders is fixed irrespective of the income of the firm—that they enter the arena of interest at once unproductive and inhuman. But if they only issue ordinary shares of small denominations providing investment for both small and large-scale investors, capital can be made available for both commerce and industry. The liability of the share-holders will remain limited as in the present joint-stock companies.

(2) Banks can also be floated on the same principle. Instead of paying a fixed rate of interest on fixed deposits, a *shirākat* bank would share its income with its fixed depositors and share-holders. To ordinary share-holders even the present-day banks pay only dividends. The same form of payment would be adopted in *shirākat* banks for fixed deposits.

Some difference in profits will have to be made in favour of shares and against fixed deposits, because each fixed deposit would be available to the banks for a year or two whereas each share would provide permanent capital to them. This difference can be easily obtained by providing, say, a double return from income for every hundred rupees invested in shares against a single return for every hundred rupees invested in fixed deposits. On current deposits this bank would give no returns. Even in the present-day banks the interest paid on current deposits is almost negligible, something like ½ %. And often enough they dont' pay any interest at all.

The *shirākat* banks would lend money to industry and commerce on the basis of *shirākat*, that is, they would share the profits with their debtors rather than burden industry and commerce with a fixed rate of interest. The process would certaily be more involved. For one thing, the banks would have to keep technical staff to examine each scheme of commerce and industry for which capital is sought, because these banks would be able to lend money only to those enterprises which are going to be productive. They cannot be indifferent as to whether their clients make any profit or not; as the present banks are. The result would be that, under the technical vigilance of the banks, capital would be directed to the most productive occupations and, therefore, the most conducive to national welfare.

Another advantage of these banks would be that the technologists would come to play an active and important role in these banks. There is a fundamental difference between the outlook of the financier and the technologist: the financier wants to grab, the technologist to create; the financier wants to earn in any case, the technologist wants to earn by creating value.

These banks would also have to keep continuous contacts with their clients after they have approved their schemes and provided them capital. They will find it to their mutual benefit to provide technical assitance and commercial guidance to their debtors. The need for constant vigilance over the actual working of each debtor can be easily reduced to workable limits by making it a term of the contract that they shall keep complete accounts just as the joint-stock companies do. The banks would audit their accounts every six months or so and see that the firms are working properly.

Thus even where the process is more involved it has distinctive advantages of its own. It provides employment to auditors and technologists. It assigns them, particularly the latter, their due place in the economic structure, providing them every opportunity to do their best. And they have much to do which never enters into the heads of the financiers.

The distinctive advantage of this system is that it is based on humanity and justice. In Islamic banking structure men will have mutual gain or suffer mutual loss, unlike the present arrangement in which the borrower works and sometimes loses and the lender never works and always gains.

A substantial portion of the liabilities of such banks would be invested in industries selected and run with the best technological skill available to it. In due course, they will become the securities behind these banks. In almost all Islamic countries shipping and textiles, iron and steel, cement and chemical and a host of other industries are waiting for these banks to provide finance for them. Similarly, they can open large stores.

These banks would not purchase interest-bearing government securities. However, in the economic structure which the Musalmans envisage no such securities will be offered for sale. They may lend money to the government for their capital investment on the basis of sharing the returns.

We have to solve one further problem and our banking structure is almost complete: How to tackle the problem of bills of exchange? Bills of exchange are an easy means of providing finance for commerce. Supposing X, a cloth merchant at Lahore, gets his goods from Y, a wholesale cloth-dealer in Karachi. Now X needs to purchase from Y Rs. 50,000 worth of cloth for which X has no money. X would write toY to send him Rs. 50,000 worth of goods and a bill of exchange which X would sign and return to Y intimating the receipt of goods and promising to pay the money at the end of thirty, sixty or ninety days. Thus X has got the cloth and can make payment after selling the cloth. But Y needs money immediately. He will sign his name on the bill and take it to a shroff who will pay him the money minus interest for the days after which the bill matures. The shroff in his turn can sign the bill and sell it to a bank.

It is obvious that, from the practical point of view, it would be difficult to extend the principle of *shirākat* to bills of exchange. We have seen that *shirākat* banks would pay no dividends on current deposits. Why should they not cash these bills of exchange free of charge? If current deposits prove insufficient for this purpose, they can add to them something like 10% from their fixed deposits to root out the evil of interest. There is, however, another hurdle to cross. If they cash the bills of exchange without interest, they will find that there is a great rush of bills of exchange presented to be cashed, all of which they cannot accept. So some check will have to be devised. It can be done by stipulating that only those bills of exchange will be cashed for which the man who has drawn the bill of exchange, or on whom it has been drawn, or who presents the bill, or all of them combined have, say, 33% of the value of the bill of exchange in current deposits of the bank. Experience will show what percentage of the current deposists will be proper for this work. Probably it will be somewhere between 25 and 50%. It should not be so high that no bills of exchange can be cashed free of charge. It should not be so low that the rush of bills of exchange may become too great for the resources of the bank.

As most of the commercial transactions are done by means of bills of exchange, the people who draw these bills generally include interest for the time the bills have to run in the price of the commodities they sell. The result is that in the present arrangement it ultimately affects the customers who have to pay higher prices. But *shirākat* banks would counteract this influence by cashing these bills of exchange free. This would tend to lower the price of goods.

Insurance

Generally, there is a prevalent notion among the Musalmans that isurance is un-Islamic. Most of the objections put forward are generally due to ignorance. There are some who say that they do not insure their lives because they trust in God Who will provide for their dependants after their death. But there is no provision in Islam preventing a man from providing for the maintenance of his dependants. So far as trust in God is concerned, we remember the story of the person who came to visit the Prophet of Islam from a far-off place. The Prophet asked him if he had tethered his camel. "No," replied the visitor, "I trust in God," "Trust in God," instructed the Prophet, "but tether your camel first."

The most prevalent objection is that insurance is a sort of gambling. If a man dies early, his dependants get a good return for a little money he has given in premia. Gambling is defined in *The Concise Oxford Dictionary* as taking "great risks to secure great results in finance". But in insurance neither the policy-holder nor the insurance company runs any risk. The policy-holder, if he lives, gets his money at the maturing of his policy. The insurance companies also run no risk. They know for certain that a few of their policy-holders will die every year to whose dependants they will have to pay the full value of their policies. It is on the basis of this knowledge that they fix their premia. So that when ten persons die out of a thousand who were insured, the money that is paid to these ten claimants is realised from the other 990 who do not die. The insurance companies arrive at this knowledge by calculating mortality over a long period and working out the average of each age. Thus what the whole thing comes to is this: a thousand persons decide to contribute a fixed premium every year for a fixed number of years stipulating that they would be collectively responsible for supporting the dependants of those of them who die before the expiry of that period. This is co-operation with a very noble end. There is no gambling in it.

There is another objection against the present - day insurance companies, which is valid from the Islamic point of view. It is pointed out that a portion of the liabilities of these companies is invested in interest-bearing government securities and bonds and bank deposits. The Musalmans should be able to' have Islamic insurance companies which do not make any investment on the basis of interest. They should supply capital for public works on the basis of *shirākat* or invest in *shirākat* banks.

The basic idea of insurance is co-operation which, as we know, is recognised in Islam. Insurance should therefore, be encouraged and extended on a national scale. Insurance against death should be left to private companies. Insurance against old age, unemployment, sickness and injury should be sponsored by the government on a national scale, so that the whole nation should be collectively responsible to provide for those who are sick or old or unprovided for or unemployed. Besides the premia, an Islamic government will have its Zakāt revenue to spend on it. It would be very similar to the National Insurance Scheme in England which covers all economic risks of all persons from the cradle to the grave. The only difference would be that the liabilities would not be used in interest-bearing undertakings.

Finance for Agriculture and Cottage Industries

Taking agriculture first, let us consider the present position. At the time of seeding, the bulk of peasants in Islamic countries need money to purchase seed and manure, or to purchase and overhaul some of the agricultural instruments, or, later on, to engage a few hands for weeding or watering the crops or later on to harvest them. On account of the petty yield of their lands, they are seldom able to have any capital of their own for these requirements. They depend on the village *sāhūkār*, or money-lender, to advance credits to them on usurious rates of interest extending to anything between 50% and 200%. Besides borrowing money on this crushing rate of interest, they are obliged to sell their crops to the *sāhūkār* who is generally also the main shopkeeper of the village. If they do not sell their crops to him, they run the risk of being refused credit in future. The *sāhūkār* purchases their crops on anything like 50% less than their wholesale market value. The result is that a major portion of the earnings of the peasantry goes to these blood-sucking *sāhūkārs*[2]. No banking structure is of any value for Islamic lands or other agricultural countries which fails to do something very substantial for these peasants. Probably something like 80% of all Musalmans are peasants. Therefore it should be the office of Islamic banking structure to liberate the huge majority of the Muslim brotherhood of nations from this crushing yoke of interest. Indeed, if it fails to do this, the claims of renaissant Islam

2. Though the *sāhūkārs* have left us after the creation of Pakistan, alternative sources of credit have emerged which, in many cases, are no less usurious.

of building a new and glorious world would be only hollow pretensions.

The principle of *shirākat* would help us here also. *Shirākat* agricultural banks should be started in every Islamic country. The capital needed for them should be provided by all the well-off agriculturists as well as by industry and commerce for ultimately in agricultural countries they depend on agriculture not only because their raw material comes from agriculture but also because a peasantry with greater purchasing power would extend the market for their goods. The government should also finance these banks because by effecting an increase in the produce of land the government would gain in the shape of increased land revenue.

The *shirākat* agricultural banks would erect plants for manufacturing scientific manure sufficient for the requirements of the area under their jurisdiction. Besides, they would own large farms in every district or tehsil to raise healthy scientific seeds of the various crops produced in the area. These banks would also erect plants to manufacture better ploughs and other agricultural instruments which may reduce the drudgery of the peasant's life.

There should be one bank for each province, with offices in districts, sub-offices in tehsils and agencies in every village.

The agency in every village would give to the peasant these fine seeds and scientific manure and improved implements at the time of seeding and debit their price which may be about 5% above the actual cost to the bank and would constitute its profits—in their name. The value of these contributions would be clear from the following facts. Experiments have shown that the produce of land can be doubled by substituting properly selected scientific seeds in place of the ordinary seeds which the peasants at present use. The value of scientific manure would be clear from a few experiments.[3] An acre of land without manure yielded 1374 lbs. of grain and 2174 lbs. of straw. Being manured with a proper quantity of cow-dung the yield was 3556 lbs. of grain and 4779 lbs. of straw. The same land on being manured with cowdung,

3. Taken from Minoo Masani, *Our India*, pp. 50-1.

bonemeal and saltpetre produced 4389 lbs. of grain and 6178 lbs. of straw. Thus the crop rose to three times on account of manure. An acre of land on which cotton grew showed even better results. Without manure it grew 50 lbs. of cotton. Manured with four tons of cowdung, the result was 80 lbs. The yield rose to 150 lbs. with 1 cwt. each of nitrate of soda, superphosphates and kainit. And when 2 cwt. each of groundnut cake, superphosphates and kainit were used, the crop was 200 lbs. of cotton. The increase in yeild with proper manure being 400%!

The village agencies by means of picture posters and radios would educate the peasants about the value of their seeds and manures and implements and would give these things to them on credit without any interest. They would also advance credits to them for buying a bull or engaging a few hands or watering or harvesting their crops or any other essential need. When the crops are ready, they will purchase the crops deducting the price of things given to them and credits advanced to them. They will forward the produce to the sub-offices of the bank in the tehsil or their offices in districts wherever the market for each crop may be. The bank would make about 5% profit in this transaction.

What this would mean in terms of human happiness is almost incalculable. But in terms of national prosperity the result would be something like this: Supposing at present a peasant grows 100 maunds of grain out of which, after giving 50 maunds to the *sāhūkār*, only 50 maunds are left with him. But when our agricultural *shirākat* banks make at least three blades of grass grow where only one grew before, the result would be that this peasant would grow 300 maunds of grain. Out of these 300 maunds the price of seeds and manures and other things would come to about 50 maunds, so that 250 maunds will be left to him. Our peasant who gets 50 maunds now will get 250 maunds then: he will become five times richer. About 80% of people in all Islamic lands depend on agriculture. If this variety of banking can obliterate privation and misery from the lives of the bulk of our population, it deserves being devoted all the finance, direction and organisation that it entails.

Our *shirākat* agricultural banks can extend their operations and increase the well-being of the peasants. They can, for instance, set up tractor plants and persuade the peasants to demolish their boundaries around their tiny pieces of land so that tractors can work and they can share the produce with their neighbours on the basis of the area belonging to each peasant.

To the man-power thus saved can be advanced raw material for cottage industries. For instance, they may be given looms and yarn on credit to make cloth in their spare time and the bank may provide market for their produce.

The bank can also persuade them to cultivate the habit of thrift, so that at the time of harvest the bank might ask them to leave one-fifth of their earnings in the bank against which they may be given shares in the bank. So that ultimately all the capital of the bank might come from the peasants themselves, and they would share the profits on the transactions of the bank. Capital provided by the government and industry and commerce in the initial stage may be withdrawn to be invested in public works and industry.

Shirākat banks for cottage industries would work on the same principle. They would advance raw material and other equipment and purchase the output after deducting the price of things advanced.

Credit for Consumptional Purposes

Though credit for consumptional purposes forms an insignificant portion of the total financial requirements of a nation, we may consider Islamic solution of it. Whenever a man needs money for consumptional purposes, which he hopes to be able to repay at some future time,Islam enjoins that the money should be provided by his more fortunate neighbours, friends or aquaintances without any interest, leaving the debtor to return the money at his convenience. This type of credit is called the worthy credit—*qarḍ-i-ḥasanah*—in Islamic terminology.

The developed individualism of man in these days may not at times permit him to ask for credit from his neighbour or friend. Generally, people should insure themselves against all emergencies. However, there will still remain situations in which a man can not provide from his own resources. For such unforeseen situations consumptional credit societies can be started which would lend money to the members. Some of them are in fact already in Hyderabad State. The working of one of them was explained by Dr. Muḥammad Ḥamīdullah in an article published in the *Ma'ārif* of March, 1944 (pp. 211-16). The following is a free rendering of extracts from the article:

The Interestless Co-operative Credit Society of Settlement and Land Record Department held its twentieth annual session a few months back. It was stated therein that in twenty years it has collected assets above one hundred thousand rupees, out of which every month loans of the value of five to six thousand rupees are given.It is based on the principle of co-operation.

This is how it works: ten men,for instance, establish a society and purchase one share each valued at Rs. 100 to be paid in instalments of Re. 1 per month...In the first month Rs. 10 are collected from the members and are given out as loan to one or more sharers. Repayment is, for instance, spread over twenty months at the rate of annas eight per month. In the second month Rs. 10 come from the members and eight annas as the repayment instalment of the loan given....Thus every month the capital of the company goes on increasing till in eight and a quarter years ten poor men collect Rs. 1000 which are lent to the members and continue circulating among them.

The establishment expenses of the society are arranged for in this way: the members pay, for instance, one pie per month for reserve fund. Besides, a tax of one anna is charged on every application for loan. When the work is sufficiently extended, it becomes enough to pay for the establishment and bad debts and also to serve as reserve fund.

In the above-mentioned Settlement and Land Record Co-operative Credit Society there are 1000 members, Muslims as well as non-Muslims. In spite of the expenses incurred by the Society, it has saved a reserve fund of Rs. 3000.

When Musalmans establish *shirākat* banks, the working of such consumptional credit societies can be improved. Roughly, about one-third of the liabilities may be invested in fixed deposit of a *shirākat* bank from the dividends of which establishment expenses can be met and a reserve fund can be built up.

A World on Planning

With the dawn of political freedom, the need of planning our way to a solvent and stable social organisation has come to be realised in an increasing measure. Considerable planning has been done to establish and extend industries and encourage agriculture. Their inter-relation would bear being re-emphasised.

Generally, thoughtful men would agree that the future of Islamic countries in the economic sphere lies in the building up of industries, heavy, medium as well as small. That is the one essential guarantee not only for national prosperity, but also for retaining political independence which, without economic independence, can seldom be safeguarded. That is also the only way in which we can provide employment for the ever-increasing Muslim population. All this is generally well understood. What is not so well understood and what should equally be kept in mind while we plan for Islamic countries is that we shall have to do something very substantial for our peasants if the Muslims are to build up a prosperous and healthy economic system. It needs to be thoroughly understood that, however ambitious our plans for industry may be, the mass of people will remain almost as poor as ever unless great improvement in agriculture is effected. To make the point clear, let us take the specific case of Pakistan. Roughly, the population of Pakistan is about 80 million increasing at the rate of about one million every year. However ambitious our industrial plan may be, it can barely absorb these one million people every year. The bulk of the population remains where it is. Prosperity would come only when we make an equally ambitious plan for our agriculture which affects 80% of our population. Our planning should be such that industries may be able to absorb our increasing population of one million annually, and our peasants may have eventually at least a 500% increase in their per capita income. We have already seen how agricultural *shirākat* banks can help to accomplish this. Let us look at the problem from another angle. Supposing we build up a huge industry absorbing a million people very year. In a few years' time enormous quantities of goods of all kinds would begin to be produced. What market would be nearer home, more convenient and more human than the 65 million peasants? But they cannot be a market unless they have purchasing power. How can they have purchasing power unless our agricultural *shirākat* banks start functioning? In agricultural countries to build up successful industry we need to build up successful agriculture! To build up national prosperity we need to build up both.

Another important point with reference to planning we have already examined in our discussion on Fascism. Islamic planning would see to it that too much of power does not go to the government, that free space remains for all individuals. Islamic planning would consciously aim at providing prosperity without taking away the liberty of individuals. *Shirākat*, i.e., co-operation, shall be the basis of our economic system. Co-operation loses its significance if it is forced from the state. Co-operation to remain what its name implies will have to be free and voluntary.

Let us see in a rough outline how our *shirākat* system would work in a proper plan. The government would borrow money on *shirākat* basis to build railways, hydro-electric and irrigation works and other capital projects. The revenue from all these sources will be divided into three portions: one going to the investors, one forming the revenue of the state and one forming a sinking fund to pay off the capital invested. So that the nation builds all these things not only free of charge but increases the national revenue.

Having increased goods and services in this way, the government can build, for example, all the roads it needs by simply creating money extending the operation over a number of years in which production is simultaneously speeded up. Agricultural and cottage industry *shirākat* banks will play a particularly important part in checking any tendency towards inflation by greatly increasing the agricultural and cottage industry output which will readily reach the market on account of these roads.

All these things the future Islamic State would be able to build free of charge. Besides a vast increase in national prosperity, their result would be an enormous increase in state revenue. This ever-increasing state revenue would meet the ever-increasing expenditure on education and medical aid.

Zakāt revenue is still left untouched. It will be expended on a national insurance scheme providing against sickness, unemployment, injury and old age.

These government operations will greatly increase the currency in the country. The *shirākat* banks would be there to take advantage of this increase in people's wealth, to attract their deposits and finance thousands of industries from cycles to aeroplanes, from engineering works to chemicals, from textiles to sewing machines, from books to scientific equipment. People would also joint to float joint-stock companies to provide the ever-increasing human needs.

In Islamic planning only the capital would be controlled at the top, otherwise the people would be free to strive and struggle in any way they like without any government interference. But when some of them fail or fall down in the struggle, the government would come back to make them rise and stand on their feet again through its national insurance scheme.

This minimum of interference from the government can be explained by giving a specific instance. Supposing a trust or a cartel is formed which, by charging high prices for its products, is oppressing the consumers. The Islamic government, instead of controlling the commodity, would encourage the floating of a consumers' corporation which would set up plant for manufacturing the commodity and bring down its price in the market. Or, if there are certain things for which scarcity prices are being charged, the consumers' corporation would turn to their production and bring down their prices. Similarly, if traders and importers persist in profiteering, the corporation can enter the field of import and trade, and by competition bring down profits to a reasonable level. This method has already been tried in Sweden and has creditably stood the test of experience.

It is no wonder that Sweden is one of the few countries in the world which has neither slums nor slumps. Her people enjoy the highest percentage of literacy in the world as well as the highest expectation of life.

The establishment of a banking structure, which excludes the baneful interest, will usher in a spectacle of social justice which would eclipse even the Swedish experiment. We have suggested how an alternative banking structure can be devised which can provide capital to industry as well as agriculture, without strangulating the healthy growth of either by the imposition of interest. The guiding principle for this change is the institution of a variable return of capital instead of interest.

Pakistan and Islamic Banking

Since this book was first published, Pakistan has come into being. Its very creation was a novel achievement in itself. It was not based on geographical cohesion; its two parts are a thousand miles apart from each other. Similarly, consideration of racial and linguistic affinities were subverted to the unity of aim and purpose, that of practising the social ideals of Islam. It is obvious that the strength and the very existence of Pakistan is absolutely dependent on translating that ideal into practice.

How far have we gone in the direction of our ideal in the economic sphere during the last four years of Pakistan? A Zakāt Committee has been formed which is examining the various problems relating to Zakāt and will submit its report to the government in due course. Agrarian legislation in several provinces has improved the condition of the peasants, though we are dangerously slow in relating ownership itself to the work performed on land. Death Duty has been levied, which the present writer considers an Islamic tax, and the laws of inheritance have been brought closer to the provisions of Islam. The Objectives Resolution has outlined the salient features of our constitution which is yet in the making. But the problem of substituting interest has so far gone by default. Banking and borrowing on every level are being made on the basis of interest. This is indeed a far cry from the explicit objective of instituting the Islamic social system for which Pakistan was created. The two most distinctive features of the economic system of Islam are the abolition of interest and the institution of Zakāt. A Zakāt Committee has been formed but so far no interest committee has been established to study the practical problems connected with the Islamic theory of capital profits. Interest is the foundation-stone of the entire economic edifice, and everything else, including Zakāt, is dependent on the credit structure of the country. It is here that Islam makes its most significant contribution and it is here that we have been most remiss in taking note of it.

Hopes rose for some time when at the time of the opening ceremony of the State Bank of Pakistan, Mr. Zahid Hussain, the Governor of the Bank, made the following observation: "Banking practices must be subjected to careful scrutiny on scientific lines by competent economists well acquainted with the basic principles and requirements of Islam. Their object must be to find out in what manner and on what lines it would be practicable to harmonise banking practices with the requirements of Islamic ideals of social and economic life. It is our intention that the research organisation which we propose to establish in the State Bank should devote special and unremitting attention to this most important aspect of our ideological problems." The Quaid-i-Azam, who performed the opening ceremony (and this was the last speech delivered by the Quaid-i-Azam), approved the proposal and blessed the intention.

Ten months later, Mr. Zahid Hussain, while delivering his presidential address at the first All-Pakistan Economic Conference, held in Lahore, underlined the urgency of studying the problem of interest: "Islam is opposed to interest, all forms of speculation and all concentrations of wealth and power, all of which are basic features of present-day social and economic order. Interest indeed constitutes one of the foundation-stones on which the edifice of modern economy rests. It is true that the rates of interest have shown a downward tendency during the last thirty years but can we look forward to a time when it can be eliminated and can we by evolving and executing any plans of reconstruction hasten the advent of that time? There are many other problems of vital import to our future but no one of them is so basic or seemingly so intractable as that of interest. It is at once a challenge and an opportunity to our genius."

Six months later, Mr. Zahid Hussain presented his report on the work done during the first year of its life by the State Bank of Pakistan. Referring to the promise made at the time of the opening ceremony of the Bank which we have quoted above, he said. "I have to acknowledge with regret that in the first year of its life the

State Bank has not been able to do anything in this direction. Our first year has been extremely busy and difficult, but the main reason for our failure has been that, in spite of serious efforts, we were unable to secure services of suitable men for staffing our research organisation. I have not yet come across any genuine economist well acquainted with the basic principles and requirements of Islam. I have come to realise to my great regret that in my ignorance I had reckoned on securing for the State Bank the services of learned men of a variety which is totally unavailable. With this experience I now propose that we should collect competent economists and learned men acquainted with the basic principles of Islam so that they should work in concert with each other."

This was the denouement. The conclusion comes when Mr. Zahid Hussain addresses the second annual general meeting of the State Bank of Pakistan. Here it is: "The Department of Research and Statistics constituted during the previous year has been reorganised. The Research Section had to be closed because duly qualified research staff was not available. It was thought more advisable to concentrate on the work relating to statistics, and build a research organisation later when the conditions are more favourable. The Department has accordingly been renamed as Department of Statistics." The first two statements quoted above contain a purposive awareness which is the more remarkable when we remember that not a single member of the central or provincial cabinets,[4] since the creation of Pakistan, has ever referred to this subject, not to speak of having done anything about it, notwithstanding the fact that this is the first fundamental of any Islamic socio-economic arrangement. Now let us see the reasons which Mr. Zahid Hussain gives for postponing research on this subject, which his earlier statements recognise as urgent. He says, he cannot find men who have a grasp of both Islam and economics to be able to undertake this research. So far as Islam is concerned, little research is called for; the directive of the Qur'ān is most explicit. We are only left with economics with which we

4. Sir Muhammd Zafrullah is an exception to this statement who made a passing reference to the duty of an Islamic State to provide a new basis of banking while closing the debate in the Constituent Assembly on the Objectives Resolution.

have to give a scientific interpretation of that directive, and it is difficult to believe that no competent economist exists either within or without this country, whom the State Bank may engage for this essential research. So the research organisation will be built "when the conditions are more favourable". What can we understand by this elusive phrase? Mr Zahid Hussain has once said something on the subject of "favourable conditions" while delivering his presidential address at the first All-Pakistan Economic Conference which may be helpful. "There are many problems," he remarked, "to which they [the economists] can direct their attention with great benefit to the country, and I will give you one instance to explain my meaning. Pakistan started with a clean slate with no public debt securities of its own. She was therefore in a unique position to make some experiments and though twenty months have passed our commitments are still of a limited nature. They will grow with the passage of time and experiment will not then be as free from risks of untoward consequences as they may be today.", Here he was clearly referring to the problem of interest and emphasising the urgency of attending to it as early as possible because with the passage of time it will become difficult to make new experiments. The conditions are favourable to do this work today and they may not be favourable tomorrow. But after one and a quarter years he himself postpones research on this subject and waits for "favourable conditions" which according to his own showing are right here and now. It is true that there is a dearth of talent in this country, but we should guard against the tendency to over-emphasise this shortage.

To return to public debt wherein Mr. Zahid Hussain rightly emphasised the need of breaking fresh ground, we find that the Pakistan Government has floated until now three series of loans, which have brought to it almost a hundred crores of rupees. They all bear interest. This then is not the way in which Islamic democracy and social justice can ever be anything more than hollow words. This is in fact the way to make Pakistan one of the many petty, rickety capitalist states battered by internal storms and strifes, born of contradictory social arrangements. The Government needs capital for its many projects of industrial and agricultural development. It should certainly float loans to get the required capital. But instead of mortgaging the current revenue to interest, this capital should share with the government the return that each productive venture gives. This is the first essential step in the war against interest which must be waged if we do not want to continue what the Qur'ān considers "a war against God and His Prophet". Supposing the government wants to build the Warsak Hydro-Electric Project which is expected to take ten years to build at a cost of ten crores of rupees. A loan may be floated in 1951, which shall not be called 1961 3% loan, but 1961 33% profits loan. When the project is completed and the current is sold to the consumers, the proceeds of this sale will constitute profits of this venture. Thirty three per cent of these profits will go as the reward of capital, another thirty-three per cent will be used to pay off a part of the loan every year, and the rest will add to the revenue of the state. To let interest weave the financial fabric of Pakistan, and still to hope that we shall be able to attain prosperity and well being is to overlook all available evidence which shows that the capitalist financial structure only leads to social chaos. We are not blessed with anything like the area or the in lustrial or agricultural potential which the U.S.A. has. Even her resources have hitherto failed to solve the problem of unemployment, except during the war-booms. The capitalist structure can only bestow the alternating miseries of unemployment and war.

Fulfilment for the people of Pakistan cannot come by imitating crude capitalism or callous communism but by initiating a new social revolution, which shall give man prosperity as well as liberty, the achievement of which has remained elusive for all the economic systems of today.

But no great achievement can ever be made without faith. Hesitation and timidity are the signs of faithless men. Even a mislaid faith is capable of great accomplishments, as Hitler's Germany, Tito's Yugoslavia and Communist Russia and China prove. The age of miracles has not passed or Communist China could never have defeated American armament nor could an unknown Tito have braved Hitler, the conqueror of Europe, in

1941. Even the creation of Pakistan is a miracle performed by faith, and its survival aganst all the machinations of its enemies is another miracle. In the face of all this to say, like some highly-placed persons of Pakistan, that the age of miracles has passed is to falsify the testimony of history. It is on the wings of faith that nations fly.

The faith of the people of Pakistan demands that we give, above all other things, first priority to discover the means wherewith we can translate into our economic life this verse of the Qur'ān:

> Those who devour usury
> Will not stand except
> As stands one whom
> The Evil One by his touch
> Hath driven to madness.
> That is because they say:
> "Trade is like usury,"
> But God hath permitted trade
> And forbidden Usury.[5]

The extent to which we succeed in doing this will be the measure of our success in creating an economic pattern which can bear the fruits of social harmony and well-being. And we should remember that in the entire range of the Qur'ān it is this verse alone which is followed by this warning:

> If ye do it not,
> Take notice of war
> From God and His Apostle.[6]

We are already at war against God, since all our economic structure is based on interest. Let us hasten to secure our peace with Him, before the otherwise inevitable doom overtakes us, which in our case may come sooner than in any other, for we carved a state on the basis of Islamic ideology and the absence of this ideological implementation risks the very existence of this state.

5. ii. 275.
6. ii. 279.